Dwight F. Boyden.

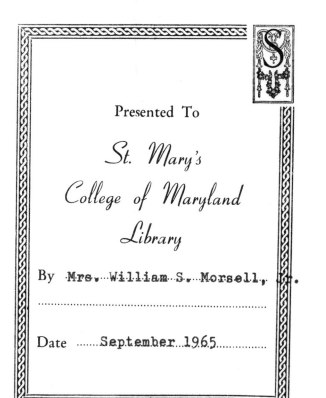

Presented To

St. Mary's
College of Maryland
Library

By Mrs. William S. Morsell, Jr.

Date September 1965

The Nineteenth of April, 1775

EARL PERCY

THE NINETEENTH
OF APRIL
1775

By

HAROLD MURDOCK

With Illustrations

BOSTON AND NEW YORK

HOUGHTON MIFFLIN COMPANY

The Riverside Press Cambridge

1925

The Riverside Press

CAMBRIDGE · MASSACHUSETTS

PRINTED IN THE U. S. A.

Preface

OF the three papers composing this volume the first
and second were read before the Massachusetts Historical Society in 1916 and 1922, the third before the
Colonial Society in 1921. By courtesy of these Socie-
ties they are now, with a few slight alterations, reprinted as read; and, as arranged, they form a consecu-
tive commentary on the first battle of the American
Revolution. I have approached the subject from a somewhat unusual point of view, which is sufficiently explained in the chapter on Historic Doubts. The military performances of our forefathers on the 19th of
April have been voluminously presented, both in oratory and in print, and my interest was first drawn to the
subject by a desire to learn what our adversaries did and
thought on that fateful day. My study of the evidence
on both sides has tempted me to test the reliability of
commonly accepted versions of certain phases of the
affair, colored, as they have been, by the local enthu-
siasms and jealousies which characterized the semi-
centennial observances of 1825.

H. M.

March, 1923

Contents

I. Historic Doubts on the Battle at Lexington   1

II. The British at Concord   45

III. Earl Percy's Retreat to Charlestown   81

Illustrations

Earl Percy *Frontispiece*

From the painting after Bettoni presented to the Town of Lexington by the Seventeenth Duke of Northumberland and now hanging in the Cary Memorial Library, Lexington. Reproduced by permission of the Selectmen.

The Battle of Lexington, by Doolittle 4

From an etching by Sidney L. Smith, published by Charles E. Goodspeed, after the original by A. Doolittle (1775).

The Battle of Lexington, by Doolittle and Barber 4

From the original executed in 1832 for John W. Barber's *History of New Haven.*

The Battle of Lexington, by Pendleton 8

From a lithograph after a drawing by M. Swett.

The Battle of Lexington, by Hammatt Billings 8

From the photogravure in the revised edition of Charles Hudson's *History of Lexington* (1913).

The Dawn of Liberty, by Hy. Sandham 12

From the painting in the Lexington Town Hall owned by the Lexington Historical Society.

The Nineteenth of April
1775

I

HISTORIC DOUBTS ON THE BATTLE AT LEXINGTON

The Nineteenth of April
1775

I

HISTORIC DOUBTS ON THE BATTLE
AT LEXINGTON

ON the 2d of September, 1824, Lafayette was a visitor in Concord, and the Honorable Samuel Hoar took occasion to remind him, in a public address, that he stood upon the spot where "the first forcible resistance" was made to the British arms. This simple assertion proved in a measure epoch-making. A half-century had passed since the great events to which Mr. Hoar referred, but his claim for Concord roused a storm of protest in Lexington. A bitter controversy ensued, and local pride and local historians were stirred to an extent that imperilled historic truth. The Town of Lexington took official cognizance of the Concord claim, and Elias Phinney, Esq., was charged with the task of demonstrating to all impartial minds that it was at Lexington, and not at Concord, that the embattled farmer fired that far-echoing shot that heralded American independence.

To assist Phinney in his work, depositions were extracted from ten aged citizens of Lexington, some of
whom

whom, fifty years before, had attended that early morning roll-call on the Common. Those venerable men, whose comrades in 1775 had been anxious to prove the peaceful intent and behavior of the minute-men, were now summoned to lend color to quite a contradictory theory. The Honorable Edward Everett, who delivered the oration at Concord on the fiftieth anniversary of the battle, was placed in a delicate position, and disclaimed any intention of pronouncing "on questions in controversy." Phinney's pamphlet on the battle appeared in 1825. Concord had old men of her own, and they were summoned into the lists to support contentions put forth by the Reverend Ezra Ripley, who published his anti-Lexington tract in 1827.

The whole dispute seems strangely trivial to us now. It is hard to account for the time and ink that were wasted in the fruitless controversy; the recriminations and bitterness of spirit, which involved the clergy of neighboring towns; the wild straining at historical gnats and the wholesale swallowing of legendary camels, and all because of the phrasing of one sentence by the Honorable Samuel Hoar. Lexington had not always been as sensitive as she was in 1824.* No one in Concord had impugned the valor of her minute-men, and it was as clear then as it is now that Captain

* The *Memoirs of Major-General William Heath* made their appearance in 1798, and contained an account of the 19th of April that was entirely in harmony with the claim of Mr. Hoar. Moreover, the Lexington company came in for a word of criticism, which will be found quoted in a subsequent note.

Parker's

THE BATTLE OF LEXINGTON, BY DOOLITTLE
(1775)

THE BATTLE OF LEXINGTON, BY DOOLITTLE AND BARBER
(1832)

Parker's company did their full duty on the 19th of April, 1775, and that, in a crisis when courage and resolution were animating the hearts of thousands of Massachusetts men, they well deserve the title of the bravest of the brave.

Two results of this controversy are worth noting: the first, a development of local interest and enthusiasm in the subject, which remains unimpaired as bitterness has waned; the second, the accumulation of a mass of questionable evidence, which in exaggerated forms has gradually become accepted as history. It was certainly a keen revival of interest that started Phinney on his task; and every one of sufficient years in Lexington must have racked his brains for some memory of the great day. In 1863 the poet Longfellow became inspired with the subject, and in glorifying Paul Revere, innocently robbed William Dawes and Dr. Prescott of well-earned honors. "Tradition, legend, tune, and song" all played their part in the reconstruction of the Lexington story, until the schoolboy of my generation, however dull in history, knew for facts that Revere rode into Concord before dawn with news that the regulars were out, and that Major Pitcairn stirred his whiskey in the Concord Tavern, with blood-curdling threats that would have done credit to a pirate king.

The new evidence, based on memories of what had happened fifty years before, served no good historical end. We know that old men forget. We know, too,
that

that they sometimes chatter glibly of events that never happened; or, as Shakespeare has it, "they remember with advantages." Is it too much to say that the depositions of 1824, whether taken in Concord or in Lexington, must be regarded in a different light from those of 1775, and that in them it is hard to sift the wheat from the chaff or to weigh the probabilities as to truth or error? To my mind material of this sort should be reserved for appendices and illustrative notes, and not included in the body of an historical work. Bancroft thought otherwise, and successive historians have been of his opinion.

By way of clarifying what I have said concerning the evolution of the Lexington story, let us refer to the accompanying illustrations, four reproduced from old prints, and one from Sandham's painting, which belongs to the Lexington Historical Society and hangs in the Town Hall. The earliest print to be examined is that of Doolittle, engraved in the fall of 1775; and it is to be noted that Pendleton, Billings, and Sandham all portray the scene from the same spot, giving the same landscape that Doolittle depicted. You know the story of this Doolittle print, one of a series of four, all of which are now so rare as to torment the dreams of collectors: how Doolittle and Earl came up to the Boston siege in a Connecticut regiment; how, in the summer, they gained permission to visit Lexington and Concord; how Earl sketched the scenes and invested them with the military episodes of the day; and how Doolittle

Doolittle engraved the sketches, and offered them for sale at James Lockwood's store, near the College in New Haven. Crude in draughtsmanship and engraving, they yet form a series of inestimable historical value. The work of provincial artists serving in Washington's army, they give us in pictorial form the story of Lexington and Concord as it was accepted in the American camp.

If you will examine our faithful reproduction of the Doolittle print, you will notice that the British are firing by platoons and that the Lexington company is dispersing in all directions. Even the magnifying glass fails to reveal any member of that company in an attitude of resistance; no suggestion of a return fire, or even of loading. One wonders why the title was not engraved, the "massacre," instead of the "battle, of Lexington." Evidently our Connecticut soldiers felt that the facts of the case, or political expediency, justified such a treatment of the subject. Then we should glance at the reduced replica of this print, which Doolittle executed in 1832 for Barber's *History of New Haven*. There could have been no political considerations to influence him at that time. Lexington was then stoutly asserting the belligerency of her minute-men; and yet, as you will see, Doolittle varied in no detail from his conception of nearly sixty years before. It is still a massacre, perpetrated upon armed but unresisting men.

The next picture to be noted, in chronological order, is Pendleton's lithograph, executed about 1830.

Pendleton

Pendleton had evidently given heed to the current controversy and to the Lexington depositions of 1824. The British are firing, the minute-men are dispersing, as Doolittle portrayed them, but eight devoted souls are still facing their enemies, six of whom are returning the British fire while two are loading. This is the picture which stirred the ire of Lemuel Shattuck of Concord, as a misrepresentation calculated to perpetuate error.*

When we come to the Billings sketch, executed a quarter of a century later, and which was used to adorn the first edition of Hudson's *Lexington* in 1868, we find the dispersing confined to the extreme left of the line, while the firing has been extended to a round dozen or more. The Sandham painting of 1886 throws off all restraint and departs definitely from the Doolittle idea. Here at last is a battle, indeed. Where in Sandham's spirited work is there any sign of wavering, any suggestion of dispersing? The line holds firm from end to end, while, unterrified by the running blaze of British musketry and the sight of stricken comrades, the minute-men stand grimly to their work, emptying their firelocks at close range into the broad and glittering target

* Shattuck's comment, contained in the appendix to his *History of Concord*, published in 1835, is as follows: "A new lithographic edition of Doolittle's Historical Engraving, first published in 1775, also appeared. In the original no one is represented as firing at the British soldiers at Lexington, but several as dispersing, and some as slain. As this would be rather an awkward representation of a *battle*, the editors, as is sometimes the practice of historians, thought fit to improve the original to suit their views of what the engagement should have been. From this picture woodcuts have been prepared, which appear in some schoolbooks, to perpetuate error."

offered

THE BATTLE OF LEXINGTON, BY PENDLETON
(ABOUT 1830)

THE BATTLE OF LEXINGTON, BY HAMMATT BILLINGS
(ABOUT 1855)

offered by the Light Infantry. Is this a true picture of what occurred on Lexington Common, or does it violate the truth beyond the limits of poetical license? I shall have occasion to refer to this picture again, but for the moment I leave this query with you, as suggesting the basis for an historic doubt.

Sir George Trevelyan, in commenting upon Concord and Lexington, says that "pages and pages have been written about the history of each ten minutes in that day, and the name of every colonist who played a part is a household word in America." He might have added that the result of this vast torrent of words which has accumulated since 1825 has been to obscure simple historical facts commonly accepted before that time, and to create a tale that does not impress one as founded upon human nature. It is natural and right that the names of colonists who espoused the popular cause should be cherished in American households; but it is a pity that, after the lapse of nearly a century and a half, other conscientious colonists, of different ways of thinking, should still be regarded as traitors and dishonest persons. The actors at Lexington and in the preceding events have become segregated into two groups — in the one the heroes, in the other the villains. It has been the tendency to portray our patriot ancestors as patient, long-suffering men of God, who, free from the selfishness and greed of our erring species, adored liberty and justice, and yearned to lay down their lives in their defence. This theory has
been

been persisted in for several generations, although Washington in his correspondence has furnished us with some very substantial evidence to the contrary. I am not sure that it is a kind thing to cast ancestors in such parts. They do not suggest the flesh and blood of a few generations since; and as they pose pompously in statuesque attitudes, and utter heroics of evident modern origin, they fail to convince, and one is conscious of the dawning in his mind of an historic doubt.

And then the villains! They are the real villains of the golden age of melodrama. There is Hutchinson, secretly forging the shackles of slavery for his honest neighbors, abetted by the malice of remorseless placemen; Ruggles, urging his wicked scheme to oppose by force "the peaceful picketing" of disinterested patriots; Sewall, deserting a holy cause merely to humor a private grudge; and then there are the villains in uniform, drunken hirelings of a king thirsting for innocent blood. There is the hint of real flesh and blood here that we miss among the heroes; and yet to some of us the question will arise, Were these men really all so bad? If some of the heroes had cursed, or if a villain or two could have uttered a repentant prayer, the whole pageant would have seemed more probable. As it is, we turn from the scene, carrying with us a sense of misgiving that is akin to doubt.

Lest I be accused of exaggeration, let me quote a characteristic passage from Hudson's *History of Lexington*, in which he apostrophizes old Middlesex as the

the Monumental county: "The towering obelisk on Bunker Hill, which looks down in an awful frown upon British vandalism, and in pious veneration upon American valor; the modest shaft at West Cambridge, which bespeaks alike the barbarity of the retreating foe and the heroic gathering of the friends of freedom, ready to do and suffer in her cause; the humble monument at Lexington, proclaiming the undaunted firmness of the minutemen and the cowardly spirit of the invaders of their rights," etc., etc. Mark how rigidly the line is drawn: on the one hand, piety, valor, undaunted firmness, and the readiness to do and suffer; on the other, vandalism, barbarity, and cowardice. Hudson wrote in 1868, and the sentiments he uttered have not become extinct. You will find them still, particularly in local histories and in books designed for youth.

It has seemed to me that our revolutionary drama would be more fairly and clearly presented if we recognize that Massachusetts was divided against itself on the great issues of the day, and if the Loyalist element were given some speaking part upon the stage. While their cause and contentions have not been altogether ignored, they have been treated with scant courtesy, and their views and influence have never been properly compounded with the general mass of historical matter upon which our revolutionary story is based. The Loyalists of Massachusetts had just as good New England blood in their veins as had James Otis or Dr. Warren;

Warren; and whoever reads the scholarly pages of
Hutchinson's history can hardly fail to recognize that
the detested Governor was quite as much a lover of his
native land as either John Hancock or Samuel Adams.
The Loyalists were not all brave or unselfish men.*
Like their enemies, they were compounded of good
and evil; but they included in their numbers many of

* A somewhat remarkable exposition of the moderate Tory point of view is
to be found in a manuscript memorandum of Timothy Pickering, Sr., in the
possession of the Massachusetts Historical Society. It is printed in their *Proceedings*, vol. 53, p. 22, and runs in part as follows: "To my brethren in
the 13 United American Colonys or States. I have lived in the Reigns of Three
Kings, who have always Protected me, and I have all along paid them a moderate Tribute as you have done. I never had any Reason to be Jealous, or
afraid of Oppression. Parliament's Readiness to Repeal Duty Acts of late years
Proves How Very Desirous they were of Living in Friendship with the Colonys. Their saying that we must be Subject to them *in all Cases whatsoever* is
like the Decree that Came out from Augustus Cæsar, that *all the World should
be taxed.* Such Declarations are always to be Understood with their Proper
Limitations. Our Maxim, *No Representation, No Taxation*, in my Opinion,
is Quite Childish, *all things Considered.* We had best look at home to find
Oppression for it has been so Great and Generall in our Northern Governments
of late that they have been Obliged to make Penall Laws to suppress it. . . .
P. S. With Respect to Mobs. There was one in Sodom when they Came
near to Break Lot's Door. There was one in Boston when they Broke open
Mr. Hutchinson's House and Plundered it. There was another when they
Broke open the Ships at Boston and Destroyed a Great deal of Merchandize
belonging to some of our Brethren in Old England. There was another in
Gibeah of Benjamin. This Brought on a Civil War in which 75 Thousand
Men were Slain. See Judges 19 and 20 Chap'rs."

Timothy Pickering was the father of the famous Colonel Timothy Pickering, who served on Washington's staff. The paper is dated Salem, June 4,
1777, nearly a year after the Declaration of Independence. It was clearly intended for newspaper publication, and it need occasion no surprise that there
is a minute of "not printed" on the back of the document. Colonel Timothy
Pickering states that his father did not approve of many ministerial measures,
but it is clear that he approved still less the severance of the old ties with Great
Britain. Mr. Pickering was a farmer and highly respected in his community.
He died in 1778. A singular feature of this document is the use of scriptural
events and texts against the popular cause.

the

THE DAWN OF LIBERTY, BY HENRY SANDHAM
(1886)

the most distinguished men in Massachusetts, who, but for the evil days upon which they fell, would have gone down in history as favorite sons. Some of them contributed incidents to our annals that might well have been recorded and remembered with pride. The story of Paul Revere, as imagined by Mr. Longfellow, stirs the most sluggish blood, and half the world knows it by heart. I can recall another episode that has to do with American grit and courage, but it concerns Colonel Saltonstall, of Haverhill, and has never been embalmed in verse.*

Let me say at the outset that I am in possession of no evidence regarding my subject that has not been accessible to historians for years. It is not my purpose to laud villains or to depreciate heroes; but as all the actors who played their part at Lexington were Englishmen, and professed loyalty to the British King, I shall discuss the episode as belonging as much to English as to American history. The Tory and the Redcoat will be given a fair hearing on the stand. The third volume of Hutchinson's *History* will be treated with as much respect as letters and speeches by any member of the Adams family. I shall assume that Mills and Hicks published as honest a newspaper as Edes and Gill; that an official report by Gage stands in the same category as a proclamation by the Provincial Congress;

---

* Brief mention of Colonel Richard Saltonstall's encounter with the mob in 1774 will be found in 2 Massachusetts Historical Society *Collections*. vol. 4, p. 164.

and

and that a letter written by a British officer to relatives or friends at home is as reliable evidence as a patriot deposition that bears a score of signatures. With this declaration of my purpose let us touch briefly upon two or three political transactions which occurred in Boston during the ten years that preceded 1775, with particular reference to their influence upon the temper and discipline of the King's troops, they being more or less essential to an understanding of the encounter that stained Lexington Common with blood nearly a century and a half ago.

It was in 1765, as a result of the Stamp Tax agitation, that Hutchinson's beautiful house in the North End was destroyed by an infuriated and drunken mob, and with it that noble library teeming with treasures of Massachusetts' historic past. A mass meeting at Faneuil Hall condemned the outrage; but, when suspected offenders were lodged in jail, they were promptly released by a more orderly but equally determined mob. When the Assembly convened, it was clear that the members were swayed by other considerations than those of simple justice. The claims of Hutchinson and other sufferers for compensation for losses sustained in the riots were laid over for one session, and then voted only upon consideration that free pardon and an immunity from prosecution should be extended to the rioters themselves.

It was this attitude of the Assembly toward the enforcement of law, its steady opposition to ministerial measures,

measures, together with renewed disturbances, which brought the 14th and 29th Regiments to Boston in 1768. A fervid flood of oratory immediately proclaimed that their mission was to reduce to abject slavery the inhabitants of the good Town of Boston. The harassed squad of soldiers in King Street fired upon the mob in 1770, and not only deprived the town of some of its undesirable denizens, but laid the corner-stone of American independence.* In the face of popular clamor, the two regiments were withdrawn to Castle William. The Town hastily collected depositions from a cloud of witnesses to prove that the fire of the troops was unprovoked, and embodied them in a printed pamphlet, copies of which were forwarded to England, with a few of Paul Revere's prints, in which Captain Preston was pictured in an unmistakably bellicose attitude. Preston and the soldiers comprising the squad were turned over to the civil power, and, undeterred by entreaties or threats, John Adams and young Josiah Quincy courageously undertook their defence. The accused persons were tried for murder in the fall, and it is interesting to compare the depositions printed in the *Short Narrative* of the Town, with the evidence produced at the trials. Captain Preston was acquitted, as were all the soldiers save two, who were convicted of manslaughter.

* John Adams's scathing characterization of this mob will be found in *Trial of the Soldiers*, Ed. 1770, p. 174; Ed. Kidder, 1870, p. 255; Drake's *Boston*, p. 780 n.

The

The removal of the troops to the Castle was a deep humiliation to the King's officers, for which the subsequent acquittal of Preston and the soldiers seemed only a tardy and insufficient reparation. The 14th and 29th were derided in Parliament as "the Sam Adams regiments"; and it is reasonable to assume that Boston came to be regarded with loathing in every messroom of the British army. Parliament held tenaciously to its stupid, blundering course; Hutchinson strove vainly to find a way to satisfy the disaffected populace that was consistent with his duty to the King; the tax on tea stimulated the popular ferment; the Port Bill was passed, and in 1774 Hutchinson sailed for England, Gage coming in as Military Governor, with a half-dozen regiments at his back.

Gage found a serious situation in the Province. Upon his prorogation of the Assembly, it promptly resolved itself into a Provincial Congress, independent of his authority. Committees of Safety and Committees of Correspondence existed in every community, for the protection of American liberties, or, as Gage saw it, for opposing the lawful acts of Parliament. The energy and secrecy developed in these organizations seem to give the lie to the aphorism that efficiency and democracy have never been made acquainted.

Upon one essential point we find Samuel Adams and General Gage in agreement: that the good people of Massachusetts Bay were in danger of losing their liberties. We know well the contention of Samuel Adams,

Adams, that those liberties were threatened by the high-handed methods of Parliament, instigated by the corrupt and selfish clique that surrounded the King. The contributions to the newspapers of the day, the sermons that thundered from a hundred pulpits, the orations in the Old South Church, all proclaim the existence of a tyranny unworthy of the dark ages in its heartless duplicity and savage barbarity. And yet Gage and his officers looked abroad and beheld a land well endowed by nature, and improved by the thrift and toil of a hardy and self-governing population, at whose doors neither tyranny nor poverty had ever knocked. The Stamp Act and the tax on tea might or might not be wise, but the uproar about slavery and oppression was to the soldier merely a blatant fraud. He resented the imputation that he came to Boston as the instrument of tyranny, and he knew that there were thousands in the town who welcomed his presence, even as an enforcer of the Port Bill and the Regulation Acts.

Then from the country came scores of quiet souls, whose lives had been made intolerable in the communities in which they lived. Their crime consisted in an open recognition of the authority of the King and Parliament. Around the candle-lit mahogany in many an old Boston mansion the officers of the army listened to tales of persecution, of threatenings, boycotts, and physical intimidation by mobs. Peace-loving folk of old American stock recited their woes as signers of the complimentary address to Governor Hutchinson : how they

they had been proscribed in the public press; how they had been ostracized and harried by strong-armed neighbors; and how, with visions of tar and feathers before their eyes, they had recanted, apologized in the public print, that they and theirs might live in peace in the land of their nativity.

There were moderate patriots in those days who deplored the outrages, and who dreaded that they would benefit the Tory cause by rendering a better cause unattractive.* In the army, with its memories of 1770, the effect was to arouse a resentment which soon blossomed into contempt and hate. Earl Percy, whose principles were all of the Whig persuasion, had come over well affected toward the Province; but, before he had been in Boston two months, he was writing home: "The people here are a set of sly, artful, hypocritical rascalls, cruel and cowards. I must own I cannot but despise them compleately." Captain Evelyn, a less conspicuous officer, writing to his reverend father, in 1774,

* John Adams was no lover of mobs. "If popular commotions can be justified in opposition to attacks upon the Constitution, it can be only when fundamentals are invaded, nor then unless for absolute necessity, and with great caution. But these tarrings and featherings, this breaking open houses by rude and insolent rabble in resentment for private wrongs, or in pursuance of private prejudices and passions, must be discountenanced. It cannot be even excused upon any principle, which can be entertained by a good citizen, a worthy member of society." *Letters*, vol. 1, p. 13.

John Andrews has this to say: "Sometime last night they gave Scott a Hilsborough treat, and not content with disfiguring the outside of his shop, they by help of a ladder open'd his chamber window and emptied several buckets full into it. Should be glad for the *honor* of the town, that they would leave off such *beastly* practices — as there are many *much* better ways of showing their resentment." *Letters*, Massachusetts Historical Society *Proceedings*, vol. 8, p. 370.

declares:

declares: "You who have seen mobs, generous ones
compared to these, may have some idea of the wretched
situation of those who were known or suspected to be
friends to the King or government of Great Britain.
Our arrival has in a great degree restored that liberty
they have been so long deprived of, even liberty of
speech and security to their persons and property,
which has for years past been at the mercy of a most
villainous mob." So you will see how natural it was
that the army came into sufficient agreement with Mr.
Samuel Adams to declare that dangers did threaten the
Goddess of Liberty in the Province of Massachusetts
Bay.

Surely no milder military rule was ever maintained
than that of General Gage. We have it on good provincial authority that his attitude was distinctly con-
ciliatory, and his demeanor toward the civil officers in
the town respectful even to the point of deference.
The local press bristled with attacks upon the government he represented, and yet no move was made toward censorship or suppression. Well-known patriot
agitators came and went, but their movements and
speeches were both ignored. In the meantime, on every
village green the provincial militia was drilling; and
the towns under the direction of the Provincial Congress were busily engaged in collecting ammunition
and supplies for war. Outside of Boston the courts were
overawed. Judges and magistrates were waited upon
by mobs and forced to resign their trusts, while soldiers

diers in Boston were systematically seduced to desert. The army became restless, and it was urged that the Governor's leniency was alienating thousands of loyal citizens, who naturally looked to him for protection. But Gage persisted in his watchful waiting, until it was whispered about in military circles that "Tommy" was no better in his high office than "an old woman."

During the period of military occupation preceding the massacre, there were frequent affrays between the soldiers and the townspeople, who, it seems clear, were for the most part the aggressors. Under Gage's administration there were no popular tumults comparable to those of earlier days, because the military were in dominating force. On the other hand, because of the discontent and the consequent deterioration of discipline in the army, the soldiers were guilty of occasional disorders, and certain young officers also became involved in affairs that disgraced their uniforms. The General had grave reason to deplore the potency of American liquor, a copper's worth of which was sufficient to convert a stolid grenadier into a raging animal, defiant of the laws of God and man. Complaints from the selectmen or from aggrieved citizens were respectfully received at headquarters, and stern punishment was meted out to the offenders in the form of courts-martial and floggings on the Common. Wherefore the army grumbled that the only element exempt from punishment was the tar-and-feathering Liberty boys, while His Majesty's loyal subjects were left to be harried

ried and hounded, and His Majesty's troops, for trifling offences, treated to floggings in the presence of their enemies. Human nature being what it is, we can easily comprehend the complaint of the army that, between the sedition of Samuel Adams and the weakness of Gage, a soldier had but a pitiful standing in Boston.

It is probable that the sentiment of the army was not altogether fair to Gage. The military problem was not as simple as it appeared to a young subaltern smoking his pipe in a regimental messroom. The effort to convince the people that the army were their friends was perhaps worth the trying. There were few instances, from the time of the destruction of Hutchinson's house in 1765 to the coming of the troops in 1774, where political offenders against the public peace were brought to justice by the civil authorities. Gage was aware of this, and in punishing his soldiers for misdemeanors he may have looked for some appreciation of a policy of even justice and fair play. Whether Lord Clive would have acted differently, had he lived and been ordered to command in Boston, is an interesting matter for historical speculation; but the time came when, under the stress of local circumstances, reënforced perhaps by instructions from London, Gage felt himself obliged to take some steps to assert the outraged dignity of King and Parliament. So the expedition to Concord was decided upon, and every precaution taken to ensure secrecy.

It was an arduous task, involving a practically continuous

tinuous march of thirty-five miles under service conditions. The Grenadiers and Light Infantry received the necessary orders; Smith, of the 10th Regiment, was assigned to command, and Bernard, of the 23d, ordered to the Grenadiers. There were more than a score of lieutenant-colonels and majors of foot eligible for the Light Infantry; and when it was learned, on the morning of the 19th of April, that Pitcairn of the Marines had gone out as the General's choice, I fancy there was approving comment in the Boston garrison. Why was Pitcairn thus honored? It is, of course, a mere matter of speculation; but, as the fateful hour approached, it is possible that the humane General became oppressed with a fear of possible bloodshed. The people were possessed with a dangerous fanatical enthusiasm, and he knew that even among his officers there was a sense of irritation, a keen desire to "have at the damned dogs." So, while perhaps it was not customary for Light Infantry to look to the Marines for commanders in the field, Gage called for Pitcairn, an officer who was not only a rigid disciplinarian, with a long and honorable record of service, but also a man whose humanity and tact had won him the love of his command, and the respect of people of all shades of political opinion in the town. Leslie, Smelt, Small, and Mitchel were all good men, but the official knock came at Pitcairn's door. Perhaps the Major laughed as he read his orders, and thought how the infantry had been slighted; perhaps his broad shoulders squared a bit

as

as he thought how the marines had been honored. I fancy (despite our local tradition) that he had a devout Scotch nature, and, as he buckled on his sword-belt, he may have breathed a simple prayer to be sustained in the work of the coming day — that it might not come to the shedding of English blood.

And now, as we shift the scene to Lexington, let me ask if it has ever occurred to you to question the wisdom of sixty or seventy men going out and forming on the level ground of the Common, in plain sight of an advancing force of seven hundred of their enemies? There was reason for posting guards at the house of Jonas Clark a few hours before; but, when Smith's column entered Lexington, John Hancock and Samuel Adams had withdrawn to safer quarters, and no one else stood in danger. Captain Parker stated, in his deposition in 1775, that he ordered the militia "to meet upon the Common to consult what to do, and concluded not to be discovered nor meddle or make with said regular troops unless they should insult or molest us." How could he expect that sixty or seventy armed men, grouped between the meeting-house and the Buckman Tavern, should fail of discovery by troops passing along the road but a few steps away; and how could he imagine that these troops would ignore them, standing as they did with shotted arms and in a posture of war?*

Captain

* General Heath commented on this fact as follows, in his *Memoirs*, published in 1798: "This company continuing to stand so near the road, after they

Captain Parker was a soldier of experience, and yet he chose a post for observation and consultation where his men would be almost brushed by the scarlet trappings of the passing enemy. Had the village been fired, had women and children stood in danger of outrage and death at the hands of a brutal soldiery, I imagine that every Lexington man would have died in defence of his home and fireside; but no outrage or insult had been reported as attending the British march; high land and thick woods, admirable spots for observation and consultation, were close at hand; and yet Parker and his men stood quietly by the wayside, inviting insult and molestation.

Has it ever occurred to you that Parker acted under orders; that the post he took was not of his choosing? Samuel Adams, the great agitator, had been a guest at Parson Clark's for days, and he was the dynamo that kept the revolutionary machinery in motion. The blood shed by Preston's men in King Street had been ably used by Adams to solidify the popular cause; and now did he feel that the time had come to draw once more the British fire?* It is perhaps a foolish query, but

it

they had certain notice of the advancing of the British in force, was but a too much braving of danger; for they were sure to meet with insult or injury, which they could not repel. Bravery when called to action should always take the strong ground on the basis of reason.'' Mr. Hudson, in the first edition of his *History of Lexington*, published in 1868, sought to justify the action of the Lexington Company; but his arguments were quite inadequate, and are apparently omitted from the new edition issued by the Lexington Historical Society.

* There is no evidence to support this theory. On the other hand, there are precedents that justify suspicion. The Reverend William Gordon, referring

to

it is engendered by an historic doubt. I cannot satisfy
my mind that Parker was the responsible agent in the
affair. At all events, it was a group of brave men that
gathered with the Lexington captain on the Green that
morning, the first flush of dawn lighting their bronzed
faces as they stood looking squarely into the face of
death.

Since both parties stoutly maintained their innocence, it is a difficult matter to decide who fired the
first shot on the 19th of April. It was a question of serious political importance in 1775, but to-day it is
merely a matter for interesting historical speculation.
The Provincial Congress followed the example of the
Town of Boston in 1770: hastily collected depositions
from all the provincial actors and spectators, published
them in the press, and hurried the information off to
England in Captain Derby's packet. The depositions
were taken for one express purpose — to show that the
British committed a bloody and unprovoked assault

to the days just before the Massacre, has this to say (*History*, vol. 1, p. 283):
"From the characters, principles, and politics of certain persons among the
leaders of the opposition, it may be feared, that they had no objection to a
recounter, that by occasioning the death of a few might eventually clear the
place of the two regiments." This statement receives a measure of confirmation
from John Adams, who, in writing his memories of the same event (*Works*,
etc., vol. 2, p. 229), says: "I suspected that this [the Massacre] was the
explosion which had been intentionally wrought up by designing men who
knew what they were aiming at, better than the instruments employed."
If Samuel Adams or his lieutenants knew the plans of the Lexington Company,
they knew also that no effective resistance could be made to the British advance. It was the rattle of British, and not American, musketry that is alleged
to have drawn from him, on the 19th of April, the oft-quoted expression,
"Oh, what a glorious morning is this!"

upon

upon innocent and unoffending men. The unanimity upon the vital point was as impressive as in the massacre affidavits of 1770; and it is only an occasional witness who strays far enough away from the main issue to throw any light upon the details of the transaction.

Let us recall the witnesses for a hasty examination. Nearly fifty men of Parker's company subscribed to two blanket depositions. They declared, in effect, that the company which was gathering dispersed on the approach of the troops. "Whilst our backs were turned on the troops, we were fired on by them . . . not a gun was fired by any person in our company on the regulars to our knowledge, before they fired on us." * This final clause, intimating that at some stage of the affair Lexington men did fire, should be especially noted, as the same hint is contained in nearly all the depositions. *Captain Parker* testified that, upon the sudden approach of the troops, he ordered his men "to disperse and not to fire. Immediately said troops made their appearance, and rushing furiously, fired upon and killed eight of our party without receiving any provocation therefor from us." *Smith*, a spectator, "saw the regular troops fire on the Lexington company," which was "then dispersing." There is no hint from the foregoing group of witnesses of any verbal preliminaries to the firing of the troops, or any suggestion as to whether this firing was spontaneous or the result of orders. *Tidd* and *Abbott* were spectators. They saw the body of troops

* Depositions of Nathaniel Mulliken and thirty-three others.

"marching

"marching up to the Lexington company which was then dispersing; soon after, the regulars fired, first a few guns, which we took to be pistols from some of the regulars who were mounted on horses; and then the said regulars fired a volley or two." *Mead* and *Harrington* also state that pistol-shots from the officers prefaced the British volleys. *Robbins* says nothing of pistol-shots, but has a good ear for speech. They came "on a quick pace towards us with three officers in their front on horseback, and on full gallop towards us, the foremost of which cried, ' *Throw down your arms*, ye villains, ye rebels,' upon which said company dispersing, the foremost of the three officers ordered their men saying, ' Fire, by God, fire,' at which moment we received a very heavy and close fire from them." *Winship*, who stood as a prisoner in the midst of the troops, observed an officer at the head of the troops, "flourishing his sword and with a loud voice giving the word Fire!" He says nothing of the command to disperse. *William Draper* avers that Captain Parker's company were turned from the troops, "making their escape by dispersing," when the regular troops made an huzza and rushed on. "After the huzza was made the commanding officer of said troops . . . gave the command to the troops, ' Fire, fire, damn you, fire.'" *Fessenden* testified that, being in a pasture near by, he viewed the whole proceeding from a distance of eighteen or twenty rods. He saw the three officers on horseback, and heard one of them cry out, "Disperse, you rebels, immediately," at the same time
brandishing

brandishing his sword three times over his head. The company immediately dispersed, while a second officer more to the rear fired a pistol. The regulars kept huzzaing till the leading officer finished brandishing his sword. He then pointed his sword toward the militia and immediately the troops fired. *Elijah Sanderson* heard an officer say, "'Damn them, we will have them,' and immediately the regulars shouted aloud, ran and fired upon the Lexington company." Finally, I quote *Willard*, who viewed the event from a window in the Harrington house, and who in some respects is the most satisfactory witness of the day: "The commanding officer said something, what I know not, but upon that the regulars ran till they came within about eight or nine rods of about an hundred of the militia of Lexington, . . . at which time the militia dispersed; then the officers made an huzza, and the private soldiers succeeded them; directly after this, an officer rode before the regulars to the other side of the body, and hollowed after the Militia, . . . and said, 'Lay down your arms, damn you, why don't you lay down your arms,' and that there was not a gun fired till the militia of Lexington were dispersed."

This, in effect, is the Lexington case so far as the evidence of participants and eye-witnesses is concerned. Upon it was based the report of the Provincial Congress. The Province also secured depositions from Lieutenant Edward T. Gould, of the King's Own Regiment, and John Bateman, a private in the 52d Regiment of of Foot. Gould was wounded at Concord, captured near Menotomy as he was returning to Boston in a chaise, and gave his testimony as a prisoner at Medford.* Bateman also was a prisoner, evidently of the willing sort, being taken at Lexington in the morning, shortly after the departure of the troops for Concord. He declared that he "heard the word of command given to the troops to fire, *and some of said troops* did fire"; also that he "never heard any of the inhabitants so much as fire one gun on said troops." This final clause was duly noted by Ripley *et al.* in urging their case against Lexington.

The evidence for the soldiers is of a different character, and far less voluminous than that offered for the Province. None of it is given under oath, but it all tends to contradict the provincial charge that the troops were the aggressors at Lexington, averring that the British fire was given in return for shots that inflicted wounds upon British soldiers. We have, in the first place, the reports of Gage and Smith; but these may be lightly dismissed as official documents penned under trying circumstances. Then we have interesting testimony of an unofficial character, in the form of letters, or private memoranda, by officers who were not eye-witnesses of the events they describe, but who portray the views and thought of British messrooms upon the subject. Upon these communications we may very reasonably build the theory that the British headquar-

---

* This testimony is referred to in a subsequent note, p. 31, *infra.*

ters

ters honestly believed in their contention that the Provincials fired the first shot at Lexington.*

We then come to the testimony of eye-witnesses, officers of the Light Infantry, who record their views in the same personal, offhand way. The most important witness in this group is Major Pitcairn. Now, what did Pitcairn say? We are fortunate in having his statement through President Stiles of Yale, as stanch a patriot as one could wish, with no disposition to white-wash the British case. "Major Pitcairn," says Stiles, "who was a good Man in a bad Cause, insisted upon it to the day of his Death, that the Colonists fired first: and that he commanded not to fire and endeavored to stay and stop the firing after it began: But then he told this with such Circumstances as convince me that he was deceived tho' on the spot. *He does not say that he saw the Colonists fire first.* Had he said it, I would have believed him, being a man of Integrity and Honor. *He expressly says he did not see who fired first;* and yet believed the Peasants began. His account is this — that riding up to them he ordered them to disperse; which

* Prominent in this class of testimony may be mentioned Earl Percy's letter to his father the day after the battle, and Lieutenant-Colonel Abercrombie's letter to Lieutenant-Governor Colden, of New York, dated May 2, 1775. "There can now surely be no doubt of their being in open Rebellion," says Percy, for THEY fired first upon the King's Troops as they were marching quietly along." Abercrombie writes : " I have made the strictest enquiry among'st the Officers and can assure you upon honor, that not One Shott was fired by any of the troops, till their men at Lexington fired on Our Men, a Serg't, a Soldier and Major Pitcairn's Horse were wounded by those three Shotts." This testimony of Abercrombie carries the more weight because it is coupled with some very frank criticism of the behavior of the troops in the afternoon.

they

they not doing instantly, he turned about to order his Troops so to draw out as to surround and disarm them. As he turned he *saw* a Gun in a Peasant's hand from behind a Wall, *flash in the pan without going off:* and instantly or very soon 2 or 3 Guns went off by which *he found his Horse wounded* and also a man *near him wounded. These Guns he did not see,* but believing they could not come from his own people, *doubted not* and so asserted that they came from our people; and that thus they began the Attack. The Impetuosity of the King's Troops were such that a promiscuous, uncommanded, but general Fire took place, which Pitcairn could not prevent; tho' he struck his staff or Sword downwards with all Earnestness as a signal to forbear or cease firing."*

Now

* *Diary of Ezra Stiles,* vol. 1, p. 604. Pitcairn's statement is confirmed in its important details by the officers of the Light Infantry who were engaged in the tragedy at Lexington. Lieutenant Gould, of the King's Own Regiment, gave his testimony as a wounded prisoner at Medford, in the form of a sworn deposition, which was incorporated in the general body of provincial evidence : " We saw a body of Provincial troops, armed, to the number of 60 or 70 men. On our approach they dispersed and soon after firing began ; but which party fired first, *I cannot exactly say,* as our troops rushed on shouting and huzzaing previous to the firing, which was continued by our troops as long as any of the Provincials were to be seen." This testimony, given under such peculiar circumstances, should be read in connection with a private memorandum included among Earl Percy's papers at Alnwick, in which he speaks of meeting Gould near Menotomy on the afternoon of the 19th of April. " Met with Lt. Gould of the King's Own Regiment, who was wounded, and who informed me that the Grens and L.I. *had been attacked by the rebels about daybreak* and were retiring."

Ensign De Bernière, of the 10th Regiment, says in his narrative (*General Gage's Instructions,* etc., Boston, 1779, p. 17; 2 Massachusetts Historical Society *Collections,* vol. 4, p. 218): " Major Pitcairn came up immediately and cried out to the rebels to *throw down their arms* and disperse, which they
did

Now this testimony of Pitcairn's troubled Stiles, who declared that it was a very great justification of Gage's claims; but I agree with him that it has an honest ring and meets the probabilities of the case. What would any conscientious officer have done on finding the Lexington company drawn up under arms by the roadside, at an hour when most good subjects of the King were supposed to be in bed? In the first place he might have ripped out an oath, and we have evidence to the effect that this was what Pitcairn did. Here was a pretty kettle of fish for an officer bound upon a secret mission, and who was due in Concord within the next two hours. That group of armed men created a situation that called for treatment. Bloodshed was not to be thought of, prisoners could not be handled on a rapid march, and I imagine that the Major was not long in deciding that these foolhardy fellows must be surrounded, disarmed, and then sent about their proper business. They had been ordered to disperse, with appropriate epithets; and, according to Captain Parker, they were dispersing when the command was given. You remember that Willard testified that "the commanding officer said something, what I know not, but

did not do; he called out a second time, but to no purpose; upon which he ordered our light-infantry to advance and disarm them, which they were doing, when one of the rebels fired a shot, our soldiers returned the fire and killed about fourteen of them."

Lieutenant Barker, of the King's Own (see "Diary of a British Officer in Boston," *Atlantic Monthly*, April, 1877), leaves this entry in his private diary: "On our coming near them, they fired one or two shots, upon which our Men *without any orders*, rushed in upon them, fired and put 'em to flight."

upon

upon that the regulars ran till they came within 8 or 9
rods of the militia." I fancy that the "something"
which Willard did not hear was Pitcairn's order to
surround and disarm the company. Then followed a
second order, but from another officer as Willard heard
it — "*Lay down your arms, damn you, why don't you lay
down your arms.*" That was the crux of the whole situation. Sixty desperate men were getting away with
their arms, and the regulars were behind in the race.
This may have been when Sanderson heard an officer
say "Damn them we will have them," referring, of
course, to the arms.

The situation here becomes hopelessly involved in
the confusion of pistol-shots and huzzas. Three Lexington men testify that they heard the command to fire.
I wish that these witnesses might have been cross-
examined by the eminent counsel who defended the
soldiers in 1770; although it is possible that they heard
aright. The Provincial, with his hatred of the powers
that would enslave him, and the soldier burning with
long-suppressed resentment, were in close contact, and
firing soon began. Perhaps a firelock in the hands of
some stern fanatic first flashed in the pan ; perhaps some
hot-headed subaltern in scarlet did hiss out the words,
"Fire, by God, fire." At all events, the volleys were
British volleys, and Pitcairn came riding in, striking
right and left among the levelled muskets and cursing
the day that had brought the Light Infantry within the
scope of his activities.

Smith's

Smith's report says nothing of any breach of discipline on the part of the troops, and merely states that they returned the provincial fire. This was the easy way out for Pitcairn, as he would have been well within his rights. But as a man of "integrity and honor," he told the truth; and it is evident that when Gage issued his *Circumstantial Account*, he based it upon what Pitcairn told him and not upon Smith's report. Had Pitcairn known that generations of unborn Americans were to condemn him as a bloody butcher, I do not think he could have been any more chagrined or miserable than he was that day. The disgrace of it all, his men out of hand and raging like a mob, the success of the march imperilled, perhaps war begun —this was a pretty situation for an honest Major of Marines.

One of the last acts of Mr. Hudson was to contribute a paper to the Massachusetts Historical Society in generous defence of Pitcairn.* He asserted, indeed, that he gave the command to fire at Lexington, and alleged, on what authority I do not know, that he had always admitted the fact. His finding was that, despite his profanity, the Major was a brave and humane man and a faithful servant to his King. Now Pitcairn's reputation for profanity rests solely upon those expressions alleged to have been uttered by him before the firing at Lexington. The Concord episode of the whiskey glass is an outgrowth of the tradition and not

* 1 Massachusetts Historical Society, *Proceedings*, vol. 17, p. 315.

an

an authority for it.* Washington has not gone down in history as a profane man because he addressed Charles Lee at Monmouth in language that suited the occasion; and yet there is quite as good a case against Washington as against Pitcairn. Can anything be more absurd than that those resonant "damns" lavished by the Major upon the Lexington militia should have been allowed to cloud his character for so long in the writing of American history?

And now, as I conclude what I have to say of Pitcairn, I wish that you might recall his features as they appear in that charming picture owned by the Lexington Historical Society. He came of an ancient Fifeshire family. His father, the Reverend David Pitcairn, was long minister at Dysart, where the Major was born in 1722. He married Elizabeth, daughter of Robert Dalrymple, of Arnsfield, Dumfriesshire, and Dreghorn Castle in Mid-Lothian. His wife predeceased him; and after his death, his orphan children were

---

* This story may have originated from certain passages in Gordon's letter of May 17, 1775, which was first published in the *Pennsylvania Gazette* in June of that year. He quotes Jones, the innkeeper and jailor at Concord, as asserting that Pitcairn assailed him with profane and abusive language. These passages were expunged from Gordon's condensed account, published in the *North American Almanac* for 1776; nor do they appear in his history. Hudson rejected the whiskey-glass story, declaring that it rested upon "very slender evidence."

The amount of cursing attributed to British officers at Concord and Lexington in the provincial accounts fairly recalls Uncle Toby's assertion that "Our armies swore terribly in Flanders — but nothing to this." The British achievement seems the more notable, as we have no record of any provincial utterance that was calculated to bring a blush to the most modest cheek.

adopted

adopted by his brother, Dr. William Pitcairn, of London, who always acted toward them with the affection and solicitude of a parent. Dr. Pitcairn was a man of rare social charm, one of the most distinguished physicians of his time, and he was honored with the presidency of the College of Physicians in London. In the Major's son, David, Dr. Pitcairn found a worthy successor, as the young man became the leading practitioner in the British metropolis, the envy and pride of his profession. The remains of the Major lie interred under the Church of St. Bartholomew the Less, in London, side by side with those of the good brother and the worthy son.

Lieutenant Colonel Abercrombie and Majors Spendlove and Williams died with Pitcairn at Bunker Hill; and yet in all quarters it was Pitcairn's death that was regarded as the irreparable loss. "The principal killed on their side," writes Earl Percy to his father after Bunker Hill, "is Dr. Warren, Prest. of the Provincial Congress, and on ours poor Major Pitcairn who commanded the two battalions of Marines and about whom I wrote to my mother." One would like much to see that letter, with Percy's tribute to a brave friend. Burgoyne was touched, and wrote to Lord Palmerston in these words: "Major Pitcairn was a brave and good man. His son, an officer in the same corps, and near him when he fell, carried his expiring father upon his back to the boats, about a quarter of a mile, kissed him and instantly returned to duty. The circumstance in the

the hands of a good painter or historian, would equal most that can be found in antiquity."* There is another contemporaneous version of the episode to which Burgoyne refers, incorrect in details, but suggestive in its spirit. It runs in this fashion: "Lieut. Pitcairn, son to the Major, was standing by his father when that noble officer fell and expired without uttering a word. He looked wistfully at the Lieutenant, who kneeled down and cried out, 'My father is killed, I have lost my father.' This slackened the firing of the regulars for some minutes, many of the men echoing the words, —'We have all lost a father.'"

The news of Pitcairn's death reached the King in July, and in August the following announcement appeared in the London papers: "Lieut. Pitcairn of the Marines (who brought his father Major Pitcairn when mortally wounded at Boston off the field of action) is appointed a captain-lieutenant of the said corps, though not in his turn, as acknowledgment of the services of his gallant father." It must have been a rare character that could arouse admiration in natures so diverse as those of General Burgoyne and the Reverend Ezra Stiles. Surely the time has come to abandon the old, baseless prejudices respecting Pitcairn, and to realize and admit that, when on the battle night he drew his last painful breath in that unknown North End dwelling, it was the soul of a very true and gallant gentleman that took its flight to God.

* Massachusetts Historical Society *Proceedings*, vol. 47, p. 288.

I have

I have frankly confessed to certain historic doubts, and have commented upon some phases of the Lexington story, from its simple historic inception to the highly elaborated forms in which it is rehearsed to-day. We have noted the attitude and experiences of the Loyalists, with a view to tracing their influence upon the King's officers, convincing them that they were employed in a righteous cause. We have discussed the long mooted question as to who gave the first fire at Lexington; and I have presented what I believe to be a reasonable version of the fateful tragedy, and of the part which Major Pitcairn played therein. As Pitcairn has long been cast as the chief villain in the piece, I have been at some pains to indicate from contemporary evidence the sort of man he really was. I must in conclusion say another word as to the alleged resistance of the Lexington company, with particular reference to the historical accuracy of Sandham's painting of the Dawn of Liberty.

Does it seem to you that the Lexington historians since 1825 have been quite fair to their minute-men of 1775? They have contended not only that a handful of their townsmen stood in arms in mute defiance of British authority, but that they engaged in battle with ten times their number of trained troops and exchanged shot for shot. Was it fair to insist that Parker's men should be regarded as something more than human, and that, modest and all unwilling, they should be forced to take a place among the Gods? Why should Lexington

Lexington have held its soldiers to standards which, if spectacular, were surely useless, rash, and unmilitary? Various declamatory speeches have been attributed to Captain Parker; but were he an ancestor of mine I should cling to what he claims to have said, himself, that he ordered his men "to disperse and not to fire." There spoke the strong and prudent soldier, who regarded his duty to his command and to the great cause he had espoused.

That the Lexington company, as a company, did not fire upon the Light Infantry on the Common is, I believe, as clearly proved as any historical fact need be; that certain individuals belonging to the company, or numbered among the spectators, did, before or after the British attack, discharge their pieces, is also clear. The British were subject to the political temptation of magnifying their losses at this point, but all they claim is that a private soldier was wounded, and that Major Pitcairn's horse was struck in two places. Now it is clear that this wounded soldier tramped on with his company to Concord, while Pitcairn's horse not only carried him through the morning, but, somewhere about one o'clock, he was still so antic that he unseated his portly rider and ran snorting into the enemy's lines, with that brace of pistols which are now among the most cherished possessions of the Lexington Historical Society. From these facts, I conclude that the injuries sustained by the British on the Common were of the order known as flesh wounds — either glancing scratches,

or

or contusions inflicted by spent balls fired from distances almost out of range. No Lexington historian has ever contended that Parker's men were deficient in the knowledge and handling of firearms, or that they were bad shots. Had they disobeyed the order to disperse, and conducted themselves as they are represented in Sandham's painting, it is certain that Pitcairn's advance companies would have been torn to shreds, and the hands that signed the depositions of 1775 would all have been clenched in death.

The present version of the Lexington story has been hallowed by long usage, and so it is a matter for some regret that Phinney in 1825 should have been induced to strive against such odds, to prove that this man or that let fly "the guts of his gun," and that British blood shed by Parker's marksmen did in the early April dawn anoint the sacred soil of Lexington. It is the more regrettable because unnecessary, the glory and fair fame of Lexington resting securely upon a sound and impressive basis of achievement. She might have cited the simple historic fact that, although on the 19th of April, she contributed hardly two per cent of the total strength that was mustered in eastern Massachusetts against the King's troops, her killed and wounded exceeded twenty per cent of the whole loss sustained. Why should a town that had done so much in the common cause have been tempted to contend for more trivial honors?

It is a singular fact that the imagination of no great artist has been stirred to portray the glory of Lexington's

ton's great day in any fashion that does not involve those
few moments of tragic confusion on the Common.
Surely there are episodes enough to fire the genius of a
dozen studios; yet our painters and engravers have gone
on tamely reproducing the Doolittle theme with this
or that amendment. We have noted the value of Doolittle's work, as performed in 1775 and repeated by him
in 1832, as giving an accurate idea of the provincial
conception of the behavior of the minute-men. He
was not as well circumstanced to depict the actions of
the King's troops, and we have reviewed evidence indicating that those smooth and even volleys, which he
depicts as rolling from the well-dressed British lines,
were never fired. Had those lines been portrayed as
broken and bulging, with scattered outbursts of musketry here and there, with officers on foot and horseback rushing about in efforts to restore order, I think
we should have something which, however discredit-
able to British military discipline, would be a closer
approximation to the truth. There is little inspiration
for the reader or the artist in such incidents as this.

Why could not Sandham, in choosing his subject,
have turned the hands of the clock back one short
half-hour? I can see a picture in the gray of the early
morning, the first tinge of dawn flushing the cloudless
east, the flicker of guttering tapers, or the dull glow
of the taproom fire shining dimly through windows in
the Buckman Tavern. The thin line is forming, and
dusky groups are moving across the Green, to take their
accustomed

accustomed places. All is silence. The rolling drum has ceased its warning, the last echo of the belfry's brazen voice has died away; and then through the stillness we seem to hear the rhythmic footfall of marching feet. The King's troops are at hand; and as we look into the depths of the gray picture, and mark that devoted band standing steadfast by the church, we feel that here is a faithful portrayal of a strangely impressive historic fact. It is an honest picture, before which Ananias would slink away abashed.

May I suggest another subject that would lend itself to artistic treatment? I find my text in the simple fact, although our historians have made nothing of it, that, when the British approached the Lexington line on their return from Concord, it was the bullets of Parker's reassembled company that came pelting among them. Surely a body of citizen soldiery that had lost nearly a quarter of their number a few hours before, as the result of the close and shattering fire of the Light Infantry, would have rested under no stigma had it appeared in arms no more that day. Discipline in the provincial militia was not strict, but it seems to me that courage was instinctive, and the meaning of comradeship and duty well understood in Lexington.

Here is the picture: Again the old historic scene, with the church and belfry. The British have passed on to Concord; and while we are conscious of the horror and mourning that have come to the quiet village dwellings, the sun shines bright upon the trampled greensward

sward of the Common. What an opportunity for an artist, in depicting the faces of those rough, determined men who regather about their captain, Jedidiah Munroe among the rest, with his bandaged wound. They stand waiting for the command to march. In a moment they will hear the tap of Dimond's drum, they will shoulder their firelocks, and, all fearless and unconquered, tramp sturdily up the Concord road, to meet what it shall please God to send them.

I admit the existence of poetical license in this conception, but I maintain that the license has not been abused, that it violates in no sense the essential fact. That fact to my mind was the most impressive, the most heroic episode of the 19th of April, 1775; and it was performed by Captain John Parker and the men of Lexington who served under his command.

II

THE BRITISH AT CONCORD

II

THE BRITISH AT CONCORD

BRITISH accounts indicate that the expedition, comprising all the Grenadiers and Light Infantry in the garrison, went out less than 700 strong.* As we know, Lieutenant-Colonel Smith, of

---

* The strength of Smith's command cannot be stated with certainty, but we know that the regiments were all far below their normal strength. American estimates give from 800 to 1000 men. An anonymous letter from an Englishman in Boston (*Detail and Conduct of the War*, p. 9) says 800. Captain Evelyn, of the 4th Regiment (See *Memoirs of W.G. Evelyn*, p. 53), says they made "near 700 men." The estimate of an officer of the 59th Regiment, quoted by Stiles (*Diary*, vol. 1, p. 575), is, "six hundred Men including Officers." Lieutenant Barker says "about 600," and he was in the detachment. Lieutenant Mackenzie, of the 23d Regiment, informs us that the combined strength of Percy and Smith "did not exceed 1500 men." (2 Massachusetts Historical Society *Proceedings*, vol. 5, p. 396.) He also gives the actual strength of his own regiment under arms on the 19th of April, as 282 rank and file. Mackenzie is a careful and convincing statistician, and it is worthy of note that, disregarding the wild estimates of his colleagues, he placed the provincial strength "actually assembled at the close of the day" at 4000. That Mackenzie was a good guesser has been proved by Mr. Frank Coburn, of the Lexington Historical Society, who, as the result of recent work among the muster-rolls in the Massachusetts State Archives, states the number of Americans engaged to have been 3763. In an intercepted letter printed in Force's *American Archives* (4th Series, vol. 2, p.440) a private soldier says that "twenty-one companies" went out with Smith. If the soldier was right, this would probably mean that nine complete regiments in Boston sent two companies each, the Marine battalion two companies, while one incomplete regiment, the 18th (Royal Irish), contributed a single company. These 21 companies at 28 men each, the known strength of the 23d Regiment, would give Smith a total strength of 588 rank and file. I fancy that Mackenzie's estimate of the combined forces was a close one, and if we assign 600 to Smith and 900 to Percy's Brigade, we are very near the truth. Mackenzie was in a position to know the facts, and had he been inclined to exaggerate the numerical inferiority of the troops, he would hardly have set the American numbers so low.

the

the 10th Regiment, was in command, accompanied
by Lieutenant-Colonel Bernard, of the Royal Welsh
Fusileers, and Major Pitcairn, of the Marines. Perhaps
these gentlemen welcomed the chance to perform
military duty in the field. There was at least the stim-
ulus of a military object to be achieved, and a bloodless success might even bring them honorable mention
and perhaps ultimate preferment. Let us for a moment
indulge in the harmless diversion of glancing over the
contemporaneous evidence upon both sides for information as to how these three brethren in arms fared
upon their way.

Smith must have realized that the success of his mission depended upon secrecy and speed. He did not
know, as he was being ferried across the moonlit waters
of the Charles, that his secret had become common
provincial property; but by the time the belfry clocks
in Boston were clanging the midnight hour, he must
have become conscious that precious time was being
lost. In proof of this we may turn to the diary of Lieutenant John Barker,* of the King's Own Regiment, a
witness who has been too carelessly examined. He
places the King's Troops ashore as early as eleven

---

* See the "Diary of a British soldier in Boston," contributed to the *Atlantic Monthly* in April, 1877, by Richard H. Dana, who describes the history of the manuscript and how it came into his hands. The identity of the
writer was not then clear beyond the fact that he was a subaltern in the 4th
or King's Own Regiment. By the elimination of all the regimental officers
mentioned in the diary, Mr. Dana reached the conclusion that the writer was
either Lieutenant David Hamilton or Lieutenant Francis Peregrine Thorne.
Since that time Barker's authorship has been firmly established. See statement
of the Reverend E. G. Porter, Colonial Society *Transactions*, vol. 5, p. 49.

o'clock,

o'clock, the hour that Paul Revere left Charlestown on his ride to Lexington, and says, moreover, that, wet and chilly with wading from the boats, they were held there inactive for three long hours, awaiting the arrival of provisions which "the Men threw away, having carried some with 'em." * Now Barker was a young subaltern of a certain well-known British type, critical of his superiors, an implacable growler, and in the plenitude of his inexperience full of ideas for putting things to rights. For all that, he is a fine fellow and an invaluable witness; and despite the darkness and his fretful state of mind, I take this opportunity of presenting him to you, as we shall be much in his company during our stay in Concord. He is our principal authority on British military activities at that place; and, although he lacks the exactness of Mackenzie, of the Fusileers,† and is somewhat unreliable in the matter of statistics, he is nevertheless a keen and helpful observer. He may have left his watch at his quarters, or perhaps

* Barker's assertion naturally suggests the query, why, if the soldiers had taken provisions with them, were they buying food in Concord so early in the forenoon as alleged in American accounts. De Bernière says (2 Massachusetts Historical Society *Collections*, vol. 4, p. 215) that the troops "landed and received a day's provisions," but he makes no mention of such supplies being regarded as superfluous or of their being thrown away.

† Lieutenant Frederick Mackenzie, of the 23d Regiment, better known as the Royal Welsh Fusileers, was promoted to a captaincy in that corps in November, 1775. He was delegated for important duties in the Boston garrison, and ultimately rose to high rank in the army. His narrative of his experiences with Percy's Brigade on the 19th of April is a singularly clear and valuable contribution to the history of the day. He was evidently an officer of force and precision, and, as stated in a previous note, he seems to have had a respect for and a mastery of statistics and detail.

he

he could not read its face by moonlight; otherwise he would hardly have asserted that the march did not begin until two o'clock, and that the long halt he bemoans consumed three hours of time. The column must have been on the move by one o'clock to have reached Lexington when it did, but a delay of two hours was quite enough to justify Barker's comments. The fact that neither Smith nor Gage cared to embalm that useless dawdling on the Cambridge flats in their official reports does not militate against the general accuracy of Barker's indictment. He lays the day's failure to this delay.

It is possible that any high hopes entertained by Smith had been dampened before the march began. Even at that early hour there may have been scattered alarm guns to convince him that treason was awake. However that may be, he knew that his last chance for credit melted into thin air with that cloud of powder-smoke that drifted across Lexington Common in the early dawn. He was not present at the first shedding of blood, but the fatal deed was the work of men serving under his command. Some of the muddled old gentlemen, survivors of the Lexington slaughter, whom the town brought forward as witnesses in its case against Concord in 1825, did testify to seeing Smith on the Common fifty years before; but they confused him with Pitcairn, and no one thought it worth his while to refresh their memories or correct their testimony.

There

There is no other contemporaneous American evidence bearing upon Smith's activities, aside from what is to be found in the prints engraved and issued by Doolittle at New Haven in the fall of 1775. In the second plate, entitled "The Town of Concord," Smith is depicted as standing with Pitcairn on the burial hill above that place, looking through his glass in the direction of the North Bridge. There is in these figures so little suggestion of the human form divine that our first feeling is that Doolittle was attempting a gross political caricature. With a broader knowledge of his work comes the conviction that, as a representation of the human visage and anatomy, this print approximates his highest level of excellence. In the fourth plate of Doolittle's, labelled "The South Part of Lexington," we may, with the aid of the key, find Smith again, this time on horseback in conference with Lord Percy. As the Colonel had been wounded a half-hour before this meeting could have taken place, we must assume that his conference with the young Northumbrian brigadier did not occur in the manner depicted in the plate.

British sources are almost equally barren of allusions to Smith; but Barker comes to our rescue in Concord, flashing him upon the screen for a moment in the following words: "Capt'n Laurie" (who was threatened by a superior force at the North Bridge) ". . . sent to Coll Smith begging he would send more Troops to his Assistance and informing him of his situation; the Coll order'd order'd 2 or 3 Compys. but put himself at their head, by which means stopt 'em from being time enough, for being a very fat heavy Man he wou'd not have reached the Bridge in half an hour, tho' it was not half a mile to it." This allusion savors of disrespect and is characteristic of Barker, who, although disapproving Laurie's management at the North Bridge, yet attributes the loss of the position mainly to Smith's deficiencies as a pedestrian.

We have noted that Smith was wounded near Lexington a half-hour before the arrival of Percy's Brigade. Ensign De Bernière of the 10th Regiment records the event in a word, but he does not treat it as a matter of importance.* We do not learn from him, or from anyone else, how the stricken commander got back to Boston — whether he continued to ride his horse, as indicated in Doolittle's print, or whether he was conveyed thither in a chaise or on a litter. Gage informs us in his official report that both Smith and Pitcairn " did everything that men could do," and that brief mention completes the sum of all that we can learn of Smith. Surely no soldier ever contributed a more difficult or more conscientious day's work to the service of his King. He does not appear to have been guilty of serious blunders or neglect. Perhaps he hardly rose to the situation at Concord; but he made an early request to Gage for reënforcements, an action that not only showed alertness and good judgment, but pre-

* 2 Massachusetts Historical Society *Collections,* vol. 4, p. 217.

vented

vented a real disaster. From the pain and seclusion of his sick-room in Boston he penned his report to Gage, and it is exceptional in the British evidence as betraying humiliation and chagrin.* It is remembered now for its querulous complaint, "they did not make one gallant attempt during so long an action." Poor Colonel Smith, to have done everything that a man could do, and to live in history by virtue of one petulant phrase!

As for Bernard, the second of the trio, lieutenant-colonel of the most distinguished regiment in the Boston garrison, he is hardly mentioned in the annals of the day. Gage is silent as to his services, but we must assume that he was in immediate command of the Grenadiers. We find his name in the official list of the wounded, for he was hit during the afternoon fighting in Menotomy; but no officer of the detachment remembered to mention it in the letters and diaries that have come down to us. In the Essex *Gazette* of May 12, 1775, is printed an intercepted letter of a common soldier of the Fusileers. He mentions the wounding of Bernard and adds the simple comment, "which all the regiment is sorry for."† This is a touching tribute, but not suggestive of fame. Let us hope that the gallant colonel's wound was as slight as his service was inconspicuous.

Pitcairn ceases to be a conspicuous figure after the firing at Lexington. We may see him in Concord

---

* 1 Massachusetts Historical Society *Proceedings*, vol. 14, p. 350.
† *Force*, 4th Series, vol. 2, p. 440.

through

through the medium of the Doolittle print we have mentioned, but we do not find him at either of the bridges, or at Colonel Barrett's where the Light Infantry were employed. It is evident that he was detained in the village for work in which he had proved himself an adept — the placating of angry citizens and persuading them to submit peacefully to the military necessities of the hour. We learn from Smith that, while in the discharge of these duties, the Major was assaulted by one irate Provincial. His whereabouts are further revealed in that preposterous petition of Martha Moulton to the Province,* praying for financial compensation for her services in persuading British officers to extinguish the fire that had caught upon the roof of the Concord Court-House. She mentions Pitcairn as among the listless redcoats to whom she made her appeal. It is probable that the Major acted the part of a kindly arbiter on more than one doubtful question of fact; but I fear that he was no match for the zealous villagers, whose capacity for bold and ingenious prevarication was quite beyond his understanding. He is not mentioned in the evidence that pertains to the return march to Lexington. We know that he lost his horse. Some American accounts have it that he was wounded and fell from his saddle. That is, of course, an error. He may have abandoned his mount as a measure of safety; but the more probable theory is that the animal reared at a close discharge of musketry and

* See appendix to Frothingham's *Siege of Boston.*

threw

threw the Major to the ground. Though neglected by history at this juncture, Pitcairn has been given a place in historical fiction. It is to James Fenimore Cooper and the pages of "Lionel Lincoln" that we must turn if we would find him on the Concord-Lexington road. Cooper gives us a vivid picture of the scene, and places the Major where he doubtless belongs, with the advance and in command of the Light Infantry. Even Cooper deserts him at Lexington, and we can only surmise and hope that, on the march to Charlestown Common, he took over the command of the men he loved, and shared the fortunes of that devoted Marine battalion which sustained more than 25 per cent of the total British casualties for the day.

Contrary to general belief, the 19th of April seems to have been a cold, windy day, with a bright sun. We learn as much from the diary of the Reverend William Marrett,* and his words receive a measure of confirmation from Parson Gordon's statement that, on the return march to Boston, the troops were annoyed by the smoke blowing back upon them. Evidently the wind was east, and from the comments of the two clergymen it is possible to imagine a typical early spring day on the New England coast, when the sea breeze comes in to break an unusually warm spell for that early season. Vegetation was certainly far advanced, trees were

* See extract from Marrett's diary in Samuel Dunster's *Henry Dunster and his Descendants*, p. 84. Jeremy Belknap's MS. entry for the day in his almanac was, "fair, cool wind."

leafing

leafing out, and probably Marrett's use of the word "cold" should be interpreted with reference to the unseasonable warmth of the days preceding. The idea of heat which tradition assigns to the day is doubtless due to the fact that a very considerable part of the able-bodied citizenry of eastern Massachusetts was at that time engaged in vigorous and unwonted exercise.

As I have said, Lieutenant Barker is our best British authority for what happened at Concord and on the road between that place and Lexington. The narrative of the Reverend Jonas Clark * has it that, after dispersing Captain Parker's company, the troops fired a volley and cheered in token of victory. Barker does not confirm that allegation, but his narrative is no more creditable for his side. "We then formed on the Common," he says, "but with some difficulty, the Men were so wild they cou'd hear no orders; we waited a considerable time there, and at length proceeded on our way to Concord, which we then learnt was our destination."

This march was uneventful, but American tradition furnishes a wealth of interesting and picturesque material as to the thoughts and doings of the country folk who lived along that quiet stretch of road. The sun was up, and all need of military secrecy was now dispelled. Many regarded the sudden appearance of the soldiery in such force as a menace, and watched their march with dismay or rage; but there were others who

* Appendix to his anniversary sermon, preached at Lexington in 1776.

gazed

gazed upon the sight as merely a fleeting pageant. The long scarlet line threading its way among the wind-tossed greenery, the play of light and shade upon polished gun-barrels and military adornments, stirred the admiration of many sturdy patriots who were to do manful work for the cause before that day was done.

"We met with no interruption," says Barker, "till within a mile or two of the Town, where the Country People had occupied a hill which commanded the road; the Light Infantry were order'd away to the right and ascended the height in one line, upon which the Yankees quitted it without firing, which they did likewise for one or two more successively. They then crossed the River beyond the Town."

This statement is in entire accord with what the Provincials have to say of their own movements from the time they first sighted the British until they passed over the North Bridge and took position on Punkatasset Hill. Shattuck estimates the number of armed Provincials at that time as about one hundred men from Concord and Lincoln; other authorities place it higher. The student is impressed with the contrast between the way the military problem was handled here and the way it had been handled in Lexington a few hours before. We are told that the Reverend Mr. Emerson was early with his parishioners in arms, and that, when the British van flashed upon his sight, he appealed to his people to stand their ground; "if we die, let us die here." Eleazer Brooks, of Lincoln, disapproved

proved the counsel of the eager young clergyman, pointed out the folly of contending against such odds, and urged that it would not do for them to begin the war. His common sense prevailed, and the handful of militia and minute-men retreated slowly, avoiding dangerous contact with their enemy, until they stood upon the hill beyond the river, where reënforcements were fast gathering. The Grenadiers followed the main road, and as they entered the village their step was timed to the music of their fifes and drums. The bandsmen of the Light Infantry on the hill responded in kind, and then there floated back from the group of retreating Provincials the faint strains of their own music, less resonant and full-bodied than the British, but as brave and defiant as any that ever was played.*

Smith's first orders in Concord were to secure the North and South Bridges, so called. Captain Pole repaired to the South Bridge with a force of Light Infantry; and then, for affairs at the other place, we may listen for a moment to Barker: "The Light Companies were detached beyond the River to examine some Houses for more stores; 1 of these Compys. was left at the Bridge, another on a Hill some distance from it, and another on a hill ¼ of a mile from that; the other 3 went forward 2 or 3 miles to seek for some Cannon which had been there but had been taken away that

---

* "We marched before them with our drums and fifes going and also the British drums and fifes. We had grand music." Captain Amos Barrett's statement, written April 19, 1775. See *Journal and Letters of Rev. Henry True*, Marion, Ohio, 1900.

morning.

morning. During this time the People were gathering together in great numbers, and taking advantage of our scatter'd disposition, seemed as if they were going to cut off the communication with the Bridge, upon which the two Companies joined and went to the Bridge to support that Company. The three Compys. drew up in the road the far side of the Bridge and the Rebels on the Hill above, cover'd by a Wall; in that situation they remained a long time, very near an hour the three Companies expecting to be attacked by the Rebels, who were about 1000 strong."

This recital of Barker's brings us up to about half-past nine, more than two hours having elapsed since the troops entered Concord Village. It was then that Laurie, the senior officer at the bridge, sent to Smith for reënforcements, and the portly Colonel responded in person with the Grenadiers, as derisively described by Barker. The British dispositions at the time were, then, briefly as follows: three companies of Light Infantry under Captain Laurie were at the North Bridge; three more companies under Captain Parsons were at Colonel Barrett's house, two miles beyond; the rest of the Light Infantry were with Captain Pole in the vicinity of the South Bridge. Colonel Smith with two or three companies of Grenadiers was on his way to reënforce Laurie, and the rest of that corps were in the village, searching for and destroying military stores. Plainly the danger point was at the North Bridge, above which was concentrated the entire armed strength

strength of Concord and the neighboring towns, a strength that constituted not only a real danger to the detachment at Colonel Barrett's, but a menace to the small force with which Laurie held the bridge. Barker says that Laurie was fearful of being attacked, and yet, as we shall see in a moment, he made no preparation for such a contingency.

The provincial numbers now amounted to about 450 men. They had come down from Punkatassett Hill and were concentrated on the open land that sloped down to the river and the bridge. They had become disturbed by the smoke rising from bonfires in the village, which gave the impression that the British were firing the place. Adjutant Hosmer is alleged to have propounded the question, "Will you let them burn the town down?" A council of war followed, whereat, in the words of Ripley, they solemnly resolved "to march into the middle of the town for its defence, or die in the attempt." Ripley further informs us that "they acted upon principle, and in the fear of God." And so Laurie's apprehensions were realized.

The fateful advance began; the 450 men of Barrett's command fell into line and marched two and two down the road to the bridge, where Laurie's 100 troopers stood at their ease. The Acton men were in front, a fact that has troubled our local history ever since.*

* For a discussion of this question from the Acton point of view see Josiah Adams's address, delivered at the "first centennial anniversary of the organization of that town," published in Boston, 1835.

Major

Major Buttrick, Colonel Robinson, of Westford, and Captain Davis marched at the head of the column. The British hastily retired across the bridge and began to remove the planks. They were ordered to desist by Buttrick. One gun, followed by two or three others, was fired by the soldiers, perhaps as a warning, the bullets splashing in the river. Then came a volley from a score of muskets, the Acton fifer was wounded, and Davis and Abner Hosmer were killed. Buttrick gave the command to fire, which was obeyed with deadly effect, and the troops retreated from the bridge. Such, in brief, is the American narrative. The affair occurred probably between half-past nine and ten o'clock and was over in a few moments.*

Here is how it appeared to Barker as he stood with his company at the bridge: "The Rebels marched into the Road and were coming down upon us, when Capn. L——e made his Men retire to this side of the Bridge (which by the bye he ought to have done at first, and then he wou'd have had time to make a good disposition, but at this time he had not, for the Rebels were got so near him that his people were obliged to form the best way they cou'd;) as soon as they were over the Bridge the three companies got one behind the other so that only the front one cou'd fire; the Rebels when they got near the Bridge halted and fronted, filling the road from the top to the bottom. The fire

---

* Record book of Captain David T. Brown. See extracts printed in footnote to page 32 of Josiah Adams's address.

soon

soon began from a dropping shot on our side when they and the front Compy. fired almost at the same instant, there being nobody to support the front Compy.* The others not firing, the whole were forced to quit the Bridge and return toward Concord; some of the Grenadiers met 'em in the road and then advanced to meet the Rebels, who had got this side the Bridge and on a good height, but seeing the manœuvre they thought proper to retire again over the Bridge; the whole then went into Concord, drew up in the Town, and waited for the 3 Companies that were gone on, which arrived in about an hour; 4 officers of 8 who were at the Bridge were wounded; 3 Men killed; 1 Sergt. and several men wounded." †

You

---

* Acton contended in 1835 (see Josiah Adams's address) that the British fired twice, and that Blanchard, the Acton fifer, was wounded at the first discharge, which occasioned the American volley. The British then delivered a return fire, killing Davis and Hosmer. Supported by statements in the depositions of Thomas Thorp and Solomon Smith, made in 1835 (see appendix to Adams's address), and assisted by discrepancies in the Concord evidence of 1775, Adams made an ingenious if not a convincing argument, his aim being to prove that no American guns were fired, after Davis fell. Barker's statement makes it clear that only the British front company fired, and that they could have fired but once.

† Gage says in his *Circumstantial Account* that the provincial fire "killed three Men, wounded four Officers, one Serjeant, and four private Men." The officers wounded at the North Bridge were four lieutenants: Gould, of the 4th Regiment, Kelley, of the 10th, Sutherland, of the 38th, and Hull, of the 43d. Gould was struck in the foot and Kelley in the hand, while Sutherland escaped with a scratch. Hull's wound was more serious, and it is probably of him that the Reverend Mr. Wheeler wrote to Ezra Stiles: "The wounded officer walked a little ways and gave out; upon which they carried him into Town; he asked his Surgeon whether his wound was mortal? yes: is there a Clergyman near? no." (Stiles's *Diary*, vol. 1, p. 552.) A chaise was impressed for his use, but he was wounded again near Menotomy, where he

was

You will notice how completely Barker's brief narrative supplements and confirms the American accounts. He admits that the British fired the first shot. He does not explain why the fire of the front company was so ineffective, being delivered at close range, and the easy explanation seems to be that there was mercy in the soldiers' hearts. Barker's comments on Laurie's defective alignment make it reasonably clear why the musketry of the Provincials wrought such damage. It is evident that the soldiers crowded into a solid block, presented a narrow front, and deep flanks that were exposed to provincial riflemen when they "fronted" all along the curving road. Strangely enough, the critical Barker has nothing to say about Smith's apparent desertion of Captain Parsons. When Smith returned

was left a prisoner, perhaps at his own request. He was kindly cared for at Samuel Butterfield's house where he was visited by the Reverend Dr. McClure, who found him lying in bed garbed in a greatcoat, a fur hat on his head. "When I fell," explained Hull, "our own people stripped me of my coat, vest, and shirt and your people of my shoes and buckles." This has been construed as meaning that he was robbed by his own men, while the proper inference would seem to be that he had been stripped by the military surgeons. He died on May 2, and his remains were delivered at the British lines with full military honors. A pathetic account of his last days is given by Dr. McClure. (1 Massachusetts Historical Society *Proceedings*, vol. 16, p. 157.)

Lieutenant Gould started to drive a chaise to Boston and left ahead of the column. He met the First Brigade on the road beyond Lexington, and later surrendered to a party of Provincials in Menotomy. American estimates are in disagreement with Barker, Gage, and nearly all the British authorities, who assert that three British soldiers were killed in the skirmish. Shattuck, in 1835, claimed three as the British loss, and on another page of his narrative we find this probable explanation: "One of the wounded died and was buried where Mr. Keyes' house stands." Shattuck did not give his authority and was ridiculed by Adams in his address. It is reasonably clear that, while the British left but two men at the bridge, a third died of his wounds as he was being carried to the village.

to

to the village, he appears to have abandoned that detachment to its fate. That it came back unscathed was not due to any effort on his part, although it is possible that he counted, and counted rightly, upon the demoralization in the provincial ranks.*

Our subject is the British in Concord, but before we turn our backs upon the old North Bridge, perhaps it is permissible to say a few words about our own people, whose rebellious activities were responsible for the presence of the soldiers in the town. In the first place, we are impressed with the prudence as well as with the courage of the provincial leaders. To refuse combat in the morning, when they believed the numerical superiority of the troops to be as eight to one, was an act of simple common sense; to attack the detachment at the bridge, when the odds were nearly five to one in their own favor, cannot be criticized upon military grounds. The controversy between Acton and Concord, which broke out sixty years after the fight, is now almost a forgotten chapter, but it has introduced a controversial quality into American accounts of the affair — disputes that in no way involve the British. While the Concord historians paid high tribute to the merits of Captain Davis, they fell short of the Acton claim that he was the only forceful spirit at the bridge, that he not only heartened but guided the councils of

* De Bernière, who was with Parsons, says, "They had taken up some of the planks of the bridge, but we got over; had they destroyed it we were most certainly all lost." He evidently counted upon no assistance from Smith.

his

his superiors, and that, when he fell, Barrett's whole command disintegrated from the lack of dominating leadership.

It must, of course, be admitted that the provincial cohesion and aggressiveness did disappear with the first exchange of shot. Most of the men who crossed the bridge in pursuit of the troops did, as Barker says, recross the river on the appearance of Smith with the Grenadiers.* Acton advocates would fain have known what became of that heroic resolve, "to march into the middle of the town for its defence or die in the attempt," a resolve subscribed to by men acting "upon principle and in the fear of God."

Under this fire of criticism the Concordians of nearly one hundred years ago conducted themselves with a patient restraint worthy of their forbears in 1775. Ripley and Shattuck had directed their shafts at Lex-

---

* Shattuck says (page 112) that about 150 men, instead of recrossing the bridge, made their way across "the Great Field" to Merriam's Corner, but does not give his authority. Amos Barrett, giving his recollections in 1825, states, "We soon drove them from the bridge," but adds, "We did not follow them." Despite this surprising statement, he goes on to say that "We then saw the whole body of the British coming out of town," and that with some 200 other Provincials he lay behind a wall with his musket trained upon Smith's Grenadiers, awaiting the command from Buttrick to fire. The British, he says, "staid about 10 minutes and then marched back and we after them." This statement of Barrett's is out of harmony with every other witness. It is possible that the 200 men mentioned by Barrett may be identical with Shattuck's 150, and that, while they did not follow the British on the road, they kept abreast by crossing "the Great Field" to Merriam's Corner. Josiah Adams ridicules Shattuck's claim and cites the deposition of Thorp: "In a short time we returned over the bridge but did not form in any order"; and that of Smith: "After a short time we dispersed, and, without any regularity, went back over the bridge."

ington,

ington, with a somewhat irritating smugness, be it said, but were guiltless of any intentional slight upon Acton, whose armed representatives had acquitted themselves with conspicuous valor at the bridge, and had sustained all the casualties inflicted by the British at that place. Under great provocation the Concord people of Shattuck's day were slow to anger; they refrained from employing the much misused affidavit; they did not protest too much. They could not account for the presence of the Acton company in the van, for that problem has always been as insoluble as it was unimportant; but they stood on the broad ground that their companies were exposed to British bullets and that Major Buttrick marched at the head of the column. That Davis, had he lived, could have held the Provincials together, is a statement that cannot be proved, as is that other assertion that he would have stood by the solemn resolve to fight his way into Concord Village. This theory seems to ignore the fact that Davis bore the reputation of being a wise as well as a courageous man.

I have wondered whether Ripley may not have innocently distorted some characteristics of the council of war upon the hill, and whether the conference that gave birth to the resolve may not have been more discordant and impulsive than solemn and deliberate in character.* At all events, no one was bound by oath to

do

* There was one impulsive man in the provincial council, if we can accept the tradition that was first given broadcast to the world by Frederic Hudson

in

do a foolish thing. The melting away of Barrett's force after the firing should have occasioned neither surprise nor criticism. These men were not trained soldiers; their military association was of the loosest and most elastic sort; they were merely stout yeomen embattled for the moment. The first reaction from the excitement of battle was doubtless one of misgiving, not unmixed with fear. They had taken a bold step: in premeditated and orderly fashion they had shed the blood of the soldiers of the King. Whether they should be known hereafter as patriots or as traitors, whether they should be crowned with laurel or hanged by the neck until they were dead, depended upon the sequel of what they had dared to do. Their fate in life and their status in history they had already consigned to the lap of the gods.

Mention should be made here of the third print in Doolittle's series, which gives us the aspect of the bat-

---

in an article on the Concord fight, published in *Harper's Magazine* in April, 1875. Captain Timothy Brown lived hard by the North Bridge, and his company of minute-men was the first to appear in arms on the battle morning. It is alleged of him that, just before the British fired their fatal volley at the bridge, a bullet whistling by his ear drew forth the unpremeditated and regrettable words, " God damn it, they are firing ball! " We are assured that this speech, so suggestive of Sergeant Cambronne's exploit at Waterloo, constituted the Captain's first and only venture within the realm of profanity. Perhaps this legend will not stand the test of modern scientific historical examination; and yet, while no advocate of swearing, I hope that its truth cannot be disproved. To me Brown's presence lends a touch of reality to that brave muster on the hill; he is a living, breathing personality, strongly drawn upon the stormy canvas of the day. We may all conjecture as to where he could have heard such language as is ascribed to him; but this much can be said in his defence, that few chronic swearers of oaths could have surpassed what he achieved on his first attempt.

tle-ground

tle-ground as it was in 1775 * — the North Bridge, the river-bank, the hillside sloping up to the muster-ground, and the houses on the ridge. From that same slope today, green acres that are still in the possession of Major Buttrick's descendants, you may look down on a scene which in nearly one hundred and fifty years has undergone no essential change; which appears much as it did on that April morning of long ago, when the Acton men came tramping out of the west to the tune of "The White Cockade." The sluggish river glides lazily beneath the replica of the old North Bridge; wildwood still fringes the banks, and its drooping foliage is reflected in the mirror of the quiet stream. The ruthless energy of man has achieved nothing to affront the eye of one who stands upon this historic ground, and who would, in imagination, travel back over the long road to yesterday. Silence and peace brood over the place, save when the motor-bus from the city, with its inquisitive and chattering freight, comes clanking and hooting up to the river's edge. Then indeed is the Old Manse roused from its dreaming by the din of infernal machinery and the Babel of many tongues.

While the embattled farmers were discharging their military duties at the North Bridge, a bloodless battle of wits was waging in Concord Village and in other sections of the town. We have only American evidence as to this contest, and it is from our own chroniclers

* The title of this print is " The Engagement at the North Bridge in Concord."

that

that we learn that the general conduct of the soldiery in the discharge of their unpleasant duty was almost above reproach.* It is true that Ripley asserts that "while in the village the British seized and abused several persons, aged men who were not armed"; but, on the other hand, he cites but one censurable incident. Deacon Thomas Barrett he characterizes as a man "noted for his piety and goodness and for his mildness of disposition"— qualities which, if now of seeming rarity, were, we are assured, the common possession of the patriot citizenry of the time. Yet this man was denounced as a traitor and his life threatened by the soldiers before he was suffered, with jocose remarks, to depart in peace. Inasmuch, however, as we know and must assume that the British knew that his son was conducting a gun factory on the paternal premises, we must in all fairness admit that if any one in Concord was to come under suspicion, or was to suffer an affront, it is possible that Deacon Barrett had qualified for the distinction.

* The allegation of both Ripley and Shattuck that the British set fire to the Concord Court-House is not only utterly out of harmony with the probabilities, but it is well-nigh disproved by the evidence usually cited in its support. Martha Moulton deposes: "When all on a sudden, they the British had set fire to the great gun carriages just by the house, and while they were in flames your petitioner saw smoke arise out of the Town House higher than the ridge of the house." (Frothingham's *Siege*, p. 369.) Hannah Moulton, as we know, was seeking some modest part of the public funds for her success in persuading the British officers to have this fire extinguished; but the inference I should draw from her somewhat ambiguous statement is that the building caught from the burning gun-carriages. This was Mr. Hudson's opinion in 1880 (1 Massachusetts Historical Society *Proceedings*, vol. 17, p. 322), and had the reverse been true, it is to be feared that the excited entreaties of Martha Moulton would have been in vain.

At

At Concord the soldiers came into contact with women. What was their attitude toward them? Read the accounts of how Mrs. Barrett fared in her house, where munitions of war were hidden in the attic under piles of feathers, and see if you can detect any act on the part of the minions of the King that was unworthy of officers or of gentlemen. In a certain room of the Jones Tavern, Henry Gardner, the Province Treasurer, had concealed "a chest containing some money and other important articles." As the soldiers were preparing to enter the room, a certain Hannah Barns appeared, with the assertion "that it was her apartment and contained her property." She was politely questioned, the soldiers passed on, and Gardner's chest was saved. In the house of Amos Wood there was a locked door which led into an apartment piled high with provincial property; but when Captain Pole was informed that frightened women of the household had taken refuge there, he forbade any one to enter and went his way. Moreover, we have it on Shattuck's authority that on quitting the house the officers left "a guinea apiece to each of the female attendants to compensate them for their trouble."

Nor was it necessary to wear the petticoat to fool a soldier. You remember how Timothy Wheeler, by his "shrewd and successful address," saved the provincial flour. He admitted the soldiers to his storehouse, where he had placed bags of his own grain alongside the provincial store. "I am a miller," he declared, putting his hand

hand upon his own bags, "and every gill of this is mine." The officer in charge withdrew his men, with the remark, "Well, we do not injure private property." * Surely what Shattuck calls "the innocent artifice of individuals" had its reward, and the victories of peace were quite as effective as those of war in bringing the King's cause to grief at Concord. The British soldier had come out hating the people; he had shed blood at Lexington; but at Concord he not only, under discipline, conducted himself with humanity and consideration, but was there hoodwinked and fooled to the top of his bent. We may well query whether Federal tax-inspectors or enforcers of the Volstead Act, operating in the old Middlesex town in this year of Grace, would prove as gullible, and as amenable to the spoken word, as were the armed forces of the King in 1775.

There was one tragic incident in Concord that must be mentioned here, as it has long been avoided or misrepresented by American writers, who, it seems to me, either failed to comprehend its importance in the battle story, or cherished a distorted notion that its recital would constitute a blot upon an heroic cause. When Captain Parsons's detachment reached the North Bridge on its return from Colonel Barrett's, the soldiers were shocked to find a comrade of Laurie's command lying in the road, with his head horribly mutilated, or, in the words of Gage in his *Circumstantial Account*,

* Holmes, *Annals*, vol. 2, p. 326.

"scalped,

"scalped, his Head much mangled, and his Ears cut off, tho' not quite dead." The culprit guilty of this brutal act of assaulting a wounded Briton appears to have been what President Langdon would have characterized as of "weak mental powers." He was known to Mr. Emerson, and that reverend gentleman, in great perturbation, whispered the facts of the case to Gordon, the historian. Gordon committed his information to print in the following words: "A young fellow coming over the bridge in order to join the country people, and seeing the soldier wounded and attempting to get up, not being under the feelings of humanity, very barbarously broke his skull and let out his brains with a small axe (apprehend of the tomahawk kind) but as to his being scalped and having his ears cut off, there was nothing in it. The poor object languished for an hour or two before he expired." * It was a cruel and unprovoked atrocity, which all Concord understood and deplored sincerely, but which the provincial authorities at Watertown hesitated to confess. The use of the word "scalped" in the British reports afforded these men the opportunity to deceive by asserting a technical truth, a temptation that was too strong to be resisted. So Zechariah Brown and Thomas Davis were brought forward, and on May 11, 1775, they made oath to the fact that they "buried the dead bodies of the King's troops that were killed at the North Bridge in Concord, and that neither of those

* *Force*, 4th Series, vol. 2, p. 621.

persons

persons were scalped nor had their ears cut off, as has been represented." *

The Reverend Ezra Ripley was most solicitous that this cat should be kept in the bag, and in his history he leaves us to infer that both of the British victims at the bridge met instantaneous death by gunfire. In 1835, Shattuck also thought it best to conceal the facts. Fortunately, or unfortunately, as we have already noted, there was that in Shattuck's narrative of the fight which offended the susceptibilities of the good people of Acton, who at once began to collect from their aged townsmen, who had served at the North Bridge sixty years before, the affidavits so characteristic of the period. In the testimony of Thomas Thorp, Solomon Smith, and Charles Handley the long-smothered facts of the Concord atrocity were once more brought joyously to light.† Josiah Adams, a native of Acton, took up the prevailing quarrel, and in a tract published in 1835 he ruthlessly arraigns Shattuck for his dishonest evasion

---

* Deposition of Zechariah Brown and Thomas Davis, Jr., Concord, May 11, 1775.

† "Two of the enemy were killed — one with a hatchet, after being wounded and helpless. This act was a matter of horror to us all. I saw him sitting up and wounded, as we had passed the bridge." (Thomas Thorp's deposition, July 10, 1835.) "Two of the British were killed there. One of them was left on the ground wounded, and in that situation, was killed by an American with a hatchet. This act met with universal disapprobation, and was excused only by the excitement and inexperience of the perpetrator." (Solomon Smith's deposition, July 10, 1835.) "I heard at the time, and many times since, that one of the two British, who were killed at the bridge, was killed with a hatchet, after he was left wounded. The young man who killed him, told me in 1807, that it had worried him very much; but that he thought he was doing right, at the time." (Charles Handley's deposition, December 1, 1835.)

of

of the episode. It is not now clear to us how the irresponsible act of a passer-by could ever have been construed as reflecting upon the fair fame of Concord; but her traducers were not in a judicial frame of mind, and doubtless Shattuck was more the object of their animosity than the town in which he lived and of which he wrote.

Acton's wrath had this result, that it restored to history the murder of the soldier. Nathaniel Hawthorne occupied the Old Manse from 1842 to 1846, and in his essay of that name he describes how, standing by the rude stone that marked the soldier's grave, he heard the story of the tragedy from the lips of "Lowell the poet." It was told as tradition, but it appealed to Hawthorne's imagination and he was fearful that it might not be true. "I could wish," he says, "that the grave might be opened; for I would fain know whether either of the skeleton soldiers has the mark of an axe in his skull. The story comes home to me like truth. Oftentimes, as an intellectual and moral exercise, I have sought to follow that poor youth through his subsequent career and observe how his soul was tortured by the blood-stain, contracted as it had been before the long custom of war had robbed human life of its sanctity and while it still seemed murderous to slay a brother man. This one circumstance has borne more fruit for me than all that history tells us of the fight." Lossing mentioned the episode in 1850, in a few brief but honest words, and Frothingham made a briefer but **equally**

equally honest statement in his *History of the Siege*. In 1858, Bancroft approached the subject with reluctance and in the spirit of an apologist. Here is his contribution, surely a model of brevity and discretion. "One wounded soldier, attempting to rise as if to escape, was struck on the head by a young man with a hatchet." We learn nothing from him of the effect of the blow, whether the soldier lived or died, whether his head was mutilated by the blade, or whether he was subdued by the flat of the axe. Bancroft was the first to palliate the young man's attack, and he leaves us to infer that the assailant was engaged in a laudable effort to prevent the escape of a prisoner. In 1875, the Reverend Grindall Reynolds carried on in Bancroft's mood while rejecting his theory.* He admitted that the soldier was cloven through the skull, but asserted that it was the deed of a lad at whom "he made a thrust with his bayonet." Five years later Mr. Hudson gave us an honest epitome of Gordon's original narrative, but concluded with the statement that the assailant struck his wounded victim "several blows upon his head, and thus ended his sufferings." Perhaps I am wrong, — it is at best a mere splitting of hairs, — but in that concluding phrase of Hudson's, I think I recognize an almost pathetic attempt on his part to convince himself that possibly the young man had recourse to his hatchet from an impelling desire to put a suffering fellow creature

* See Reynolds's tract on Concord Fight published in Boston, 1875. This theory was based on a statement made by Chaplain Thaxter in his old age.

out

out of misery. The real trouble with Hudson's statement is that there is nothing to show that the soldier's wound was mortal; and the British assertion, that he was "not quite dead" when found, is confirmed by Gordon's admission that "the poor object languished for an hour or two before he expired." These evasions and theories of our nineteenth-century writers are submitted for their psychological rather than for their historical interest. We may rest assured that the Reverend Mr. Emerson knew the facts, and, had there been extenuating circumstances of the sort I have quoted, he would have communicated them to Gordon in 1775.

The importance of this regrettable episode lies in the influence it exerted upon the British morale on the 19th of April, and, through not unnatural distortions and exaggerations, upon public opinion in England. How could it have been otherwise? The one hundred witnesses of Parsons's command were soon mingling with their comrades in the village, and the gruesome tale was passed from mouth to mouth in all sorts of exaggerated forms. You read of it in the reports of Smith and Percy, in Gage's letter to Trumbull, in his official report to the War Office in London, and in the Parliamentary records. You find it, too, in private letters of British officers and soldiers. We may regret that a frank statement of the facts was not forthcoming from the Provincial Congress. This would have cleared up the charges or robbed them of their sting; but for the British

British soldier in Concord no explanation was possible, and when about noon the orders rang out that put the column in motion on its return march to Boston, the sickening conviction had spread throughout the ranks that the Americans "scalped" the wounded. With rage and horror in their hearts, the Grenadiers and Light Infantry passed out of Concord into Lexington road. All along the high ground above, the provincial minute-men were gathering, and they looked down in anger upon the ruthless hirelings of the Crown, whose hands were stained with American blood that cried out for vengeance. The sort of resentment upon which brutality thrives was raging in the hearts of men on both sides as the British took up their march.

American annals teem with picturesque incidents that have to do with that happy hunting from Concord to Lexington, and tablets placed along the old battle-road commemorate many real and fancied episodes of the day. The American scheme of attack was, of course, a happening, and not the result of a prearranged plan. Its effectiveness may well have been a surprise to them, as it was a matter of consternation to their enemy. No one can say how many of the armed men gathered in Concord entered upon the pursuit; but it is probable that, after Merriam's Corner had been passed, the numerical superiority was with the Provincials. Minute-men diverted from their march to Concord by the sound of firing closed in upon the Lexington road and secreted themselves in the underbrush and behind other favorable

ble cover. Fresh companies were constantly arriving. As the men grew bolder, they entered houses and fired from within and behind them. The British rear guard was much annoyed by the fire from buildings which, during the passage of the column, had appeared to be deserted.

As the troops approached the Lexington line, they were opposed by more than twice their number. Here they encountered anew the indomitable Lexington company, and here Jedidiah Munroe, who had been wounded on the Common in the morning, met a soldier's death. Smith's flank guards, whose early operations had been effective, now began to fail from sheer exhaustion. The British commander had pinned his faith to the reënforcements for which he had appealed in the early morning hours, and their non-appearance filled him with anxiety and dismay. British evidence makes it clear that the soldiers threw away their fire without judgment, with no enemy in sight; and in the extraordinary conditions prevailing, the officers seem to have been powerless to prevent this waste. These soldiers were maddened by the galling fire they sustained from unseen enemies, and the dread of "scalping" was always in their minds. Yet no charge of cruelty lies against them, and we know that such of their wounded as fell into provincial hands were treated with humanity and consideration. All angered as they were, these warring men of common British ancestry maintained a clean, if bitter, fight along that six miles of road.

Smith

Smith, seeing no way of crippling his enemy, tried to speed up his march, and prayed with lessening faith for the arrival of the long-expected succor. He was wounded at a critical moment. The column was then approaching Lexington Village. Its effective strength had been seriously reduced by death and wounds, panic and insubordination threatened, and the ammunition was nearly exhausted. The officers tell plain, straightforward stories in the diaries and letters that have been brought to light; they show no disposition to minimize the peril in which they stood. Hope of assistance had well-nigh vanished, and the surrender or dispersal of the entire detachment seemed imminent.

Then, almost in the twinkling of an eye, the situation changed. The provincial fire, which had been growing closer and more deadly with every moment, suddenly waned, then almost ceased, and the Light Infantry, passing hurriedly on by Lexington Common, found themselves looking into the promised land. It was no mirage or optical illusion that met their half-doubting gaze, but a scarlet line that stretched its imposing length all along the rising ground in front — the battle-line of the First Brigade. Above the steel-fringed ranks of infantry the standards of three famous British regiments streamed out in the fresh breeze. A cloud of smoke billowed above the tree-tops, and the roar of a six-pounder, echoing and reverberating among the woods and hills, proclaimed that the Royal Artillery was in the field. What wonder that the weary,
tortured

tortured soldiery broke into shouts and cheers as they first beheld Earl Percy and his men? After despondency and dread, they tasted real exaltation that was akin to the joy of victory. The Provincials, robbed of their prey, experienced the disappointment and chagrin that is born of a sense of defeat. There was to be hard fighting for all these men of kindred blood before the setting of the sun; but with the first cannon-shot the curtain falls upon what for the King's troops was the critical period of that April battle-day.

III

EARL PERCY'S RETREAT TO CHARLESTOWN

EARL PERCY'S RETREAT TO CHARLESTOWN

THE casual observer who visits Lexington to-day might carry away the idea that Percy was the presiding genius of the place. While he made but one visit to the town, and that of a flying nature, he has always been numbered as among its distinguished guests. He received a warm, if not a cordial, reception; and if he did not endear himself to the townsfolk of the time, he might have pleaded in defence that when in Rome he did as the Romans did. The old Munroe Tavern has, on quite insufficient grounds, been christened "Earl Percy's Headquarters," and the renovated rooms of the ancient hostelry contain, among other battle relics, prints and documents that have to do with him. The pleasant road winding up the slope behind the tavern now bears his name; a gun-site chosen by his artillerymen is marked by a rude imitation of a cannon carved from solid rock; while in the Cary Library hangs his portrait in oil, a gift to the town from a modern Duke of Northumberland.

There is far more in Lexington suggestive of Percy than of Captain Parker. The bronze effigy of the Minute-Man gazing steadfastly down the old Boston road idealizes

idealizes the spirit of Parker's command, but in no sense portrays the visage of Parker himself. On the Common, cut in stone, are certain words attributed to Parker which we may hope, nay believe, that he never uttered. These are almost the only reminders of the Lexington Captain that confront the tripper on his hasty rounds. I would not convey the impression that Lexington has proved recreant to its Revolutionary traditions, or that it has turned to the worship of false idols. At a town meeting called a few years ago to consider the naming of "Percy Road," the spirit of 1775 blazed forth in unmistakable fervor. That there was a contest proved that the citizens were keenly alive to their historic inheritance, while the final result reflected great credit upon their sportsmanship and common sense.

Let us now try to imagine ourselves as standing in old Lexington on that bright April afternoon one hundred and forty-eight years ago. I will ask you to believe that the First Brigade has been for more than five hours on the march; that the precocious lad in Roxbury has discharged with credit his declamation of the suggestive lines from the "Ballad of Chevy Chase"; that the absent-minded tutor in Harvard Square has directed Percy along the right road and become one of the most innocent of offenders; that Percy has held his informing interview with the wounded Gould as he reclined in his chaise; and that now, at half-past two in the afternoon, the whole brigade stands drawn up in line

line of battle on the high ground east of Lexington Village.*

We should also refresh our memories as to certain well-known facts: namely, that the Brigade came out in response to Smith's early warning that the country was aroused; that there was a delay in starting, because of a staff blunder thoroughly characteristic of the military annals of the Anglo-Saxon race;† that the long road through Roxbury was followed because all boats for river-transportation were still moored on the Cam-

---

* The erroneous idea that the Brigade received Smith's fugitives within a hollow square at Lexington apparently originated with Stedman, the British historian, in 1794. (*History of the American War*, vol. 1, p. 119.) Percy states in his report to Gage that he "drew up the Brigade on a height." (*Letters*, 1902, p. 50.) Lieutenant Mackenzie gives us the authoritative account of the disposition of the troops at Lexington, and makes it clear that they stood in line of battle throughout the halt. He states that the Grenadiers and Light Infantry "retired and formed behind the brigade." (2 Massachusetts Historical Society *Proceedings*, vol. 5, p. 392.)

† This blunder is thus described in a letter dated Boston, July 5, 1775:

"The general ordered the first brigade under arms at four in the morning; these orders the evening before were carried to the brigade major's; he was not at home; the orders were left; no enquiry was made after him; he came home late; his servant forgot to tell him there was a letter on his table; four o'clock came; no brigade appeared; at five o'clock an express from Smith desiring a reënforcement produced an enquiry; the above discovery was made; at six o'clock part of the brigade got on the parade; there they waited, expecting the marines; at seven, no marines appearing, another enquiry commenced; they said they had received no orders; it was asserted they had; in the altercation it came out that the order had been addressed to Major Pitcairn who commanded the marines and left at his quarters, though the gentleman concerned ought to have recollected that Pitcairn had been dispatched the evening before with the grenadiers and light infantry under Lieut. Col. Smith. This double mistake lost us from four till nine o'clock, the time we marched off to support Col. Smith." (*Detail and Conduct of the American War*, 3d ed., London, 1780, p. 10.) This letter is found in an earlier but undated edition of the same pamphlet, entitled *A View of the Evidence relative to the Conduct of the American War*, etc., London, p. 72.

bridge

bridge side of the Charles to await Smith's return; that the Brigade was made up of the 4th, 23d, and 47th Regiments of Foot,* the First Battalion of Marines, and a detachment of the Royal Artillery; and that the total strength of the command was something less than one thousand men.†

In considering Earl Percy's activities, let us first review briefly his military conduct in the handling of a difficult problem, and then consider with more care the charges of brutality and vandalism that have been levelled against him. Perhaps at the outset it will be well to glance at the fourth print of Doolittle's well-known series, entitled "A View of the South Part of Lexington." This portrays the meeting of Smith and Percy near the junction of the Boston and Woburn roads. The Provincials appear in the foreground, huddled behind the walls that line the last-named thoroughfare. The Brigade is still in route formation, facing the Common, while its flank guards are seen at work clearing up the hillsides. A field-piece is just going into action, and Smith's jaded column can be seen in the background, moving off by their right flank to gain the rear of the Brigade. The British sol-

---

* The 4th Regiment was better known as "The King's Own," and the 23d as "The Royal Welsh Fusileers."

† The Boston garrison had been brigaded as follows:

    First Brigade (Percy), 4th, 23d, and 47th Regiments; First Battalion of Marines.

    Second Brigade (Pigot), 5th, 38th, and 52d Regiments.

    Third Brigade (Jones), 10th, 43d, and 59th Regiments; 3 companies of the 18th and 2 companies of the 65th regiments.

diers

diers appear more like birds than men; and once again the thought recurs that Doolittle has attempted a political caricature in portraying them as birds of prey. You will note, however, that the minute-men in the plate present the same aspect, and that the phenomenon is all traceable to Doolittle's faulty conception of the cut of a military coat. From which we may infer that, if Doolittle was a bad engraver, he would have been a greater failure as a tailor. With a magnifying-glass we can make out Percy and Smith on horseback, in close consultation. That they appear like scarlet vultures does not detract from the value or realism of the view. But the really dominant features in Doolittle's engraving are the smoke and flames that hang in rigid, petrified masses above three burning houses. It has been asserted that the greatest British devastation in Lexington was wrought almost in Percy's presence, and Doolittle's print supplies powerful support to the charge.

The work of Doolittle in his series of Lexington prints is invaluable for its portrayal of local topography and for the record it gives of the current idea of the provincial dispositions and activities. On the other hand, we should remember that his conception of British alignments must in the nature of things be less dependable. It is doubtful if Smith with a ball in his leg was able to sit his horse while he conferred with Percy, as indicated in the print. To represent the Brigade as moving along the road in column of twos at this juncture is, of course, wholly inaccurate. We know on the clearest

clearest evidence that at the time the Grenadiers and Light Infantry were passing through Lexington Village, Percy had formed in line of battle, and was swinging his six-pounders into position. It is probable, however, that, as depicted in the print, Smith did move by his right flank, passing through or around Percy's left to safety and shelter.

Percy had never imagined such a situation as he found at Lexington. He possessed military experience; he had served under Ferdinand of Brunswick, had fought at Minden, and was well versed in military science as it was then practised on the Continent. But now he found himself for the first time in a supreme command, facing a problem that was unique and bewildering, one for which European military formulas afforded no satisfactory solution. Had he been in telephonic communication with Boston, he might have been weak enough to call up General Gage and seek counsel from that timid and anxious man. Lacking this facility, he had to rely upon his military instinct and resourcefulness. He knew that the aim of his adversaries was to destroy or capture his command, and that his plain duty was to conduct that command safely to Boston with the minimum of loss. He was unrestrained by any of those political considerations that benumbed the royal commanders in the later years of the Revolution. He believed that war had begun, and that not only was he powerless to avert the shedding of blood, but the safety of his men would require the infliction of

of the maximum of damage upon his foe. In this conviction he girded his loins and hardened his heart for
the task before him. There can be no doubt that he
listened to Smith's story and probably to Pitcairn's and
Bernard's too. We know what he learned as well as if
he had recorded it in black and white for the benefit
of posterity. The troops had marched from Concord
under an incessant fire from unseen enemies concealed
in houses and behind walls. Houses apparently deserted
had been found by the rear guard to be full of armed
enemies. The Americans had reverted to the methods
of Indian warfare, not omitting — so it was alleged —
the scalping of the wounded.

The first necessity of the case was to secure for
Smith's shattered detachment some brief opportunity
to recuperate from the fatigue and strain of twelve
hours' rough campaigning. So, ordering Bernard and
Pitcairn to look well to their men and to care for the
wounded at Munroe's Tavern, Percy proceeded to
clear away a zone that should be free from rebel musketry. His orders received prompt and ready obedi-
ence. Strong flank guards clambered along the slopes
above the road, the field-pieces began to bark, and a
round shot went crashing and splintering through the
meeting-house of the Reverend Jonas Clark. There
has been a persistent effort to include this shot in the
list of Percy's barbarities. The Reverend Abel Muz-
zey, in 1877, in recording his boyish memories of the
aged men who had stood with Parker at Lexington,
refers

refers to this event as an "act of desecration,"* and quotes from the anniversary sermon of the Reverend Isaac Morrill, preached at Lexington in 1780, wherein he also emphasizes the impiety of the deed.† Inasmuch, however, as British witnesses record a provincial concentration within the shadow of the sacred edifice,‡ as we know that the place was used for the storage of the town supply of powder, and that no less a person than Colonel Baldwin, of Woburn, was narrowly missed by the flying ball, I think we are warranted in including this achievement of the Royal Artillery as among the justifiable acts of war.

"Houses and walls" — how many times had these words been dinned into Percy's ears during the scant sixty minutes of his halt! They were doubtless in his mind when his glance fell upon Deacon Loring's buildings and his well-laid stone walls. Perhaps the windows raked the road at too advantageous an angle; perhaps the structures interfered with the range of his artillery; at all events, it is certain that the walls offered tempting cover for a hostile force. So the command was given, and Deacon Loring's buildings went up in

* *New England Historic-Genealogical Register*, vol. 31, p. 382.

† "Let the mark of British tyranny, made in this house of God, remain till time itself shall consume the fabrick, and it moulders into dust." ("Faith in Divine Providence, the great support of God's People in perilous times." A Sermon, etc., 1780, p. 26.)

‡ "They appeared most numerous in the road near the Church, and in a wood in the front and on the left flank of the line where our Regiment was posted. A few Cannon shot were fired at those on & near the road, which dispersed them." (Mackenzie, 2 Massachusetts Historical Society *Proceedings*, vol 5, p. 392.)

flames

flames and two hundred rods of his stone wall came down in dust. Two other dwellings also were fired, and Percy sat his white charger, watching the operations of flank guards, artillery, and uniformed incendiaries, and grimly approved it all.

It has been customary to ascribe these acts to the revengeful vandalism of a frenzied and humiliated soldiery, and to allege that by condoning such outrages Percy made himself an accessory after the fact. But surely it is a more sensible theory to assume that the damage was wrought by Percy's express command, as a necessary measure of protection for his men. We must remember that the Brigade still stood in battle-line, that straggling under such conditions was well-nigh impossible, and that there is not the slightest reason to suppose that these men were infected with any fury or that they were not under perfect control. The Grenadiers and Light Infantry had gone to the rear, and must have been concentrated in the vicinity of the tavern. I am very strongly of the opinion that, being in close proximity to Landlord Munroe's bar, they were giving their officers a thoroughly bad quarter of an hour. It is evident that the burning of houses and the destruction of walls were simultaneous parts of an orderly military operation. Smith's soldiers, described by Stedman as so exhausted that they lay on the ground, "their tongues hanging out of their mouths, like those of dogs after a chase,"* could certainly be trusted not to bestir

* *History of the American War* (1794), vol. I, p. 118.

themselves

themselves against stone walls; nor is it more reasonable to assume that the men of the Brigade, after a forced march of sixteen miles, with the knowledge that there were many more to go, would have entered upon any such athletic enterprise except by imperative order. You may demur at this theory, and question my decision to regard the destruction wrought by the troops during the halt in Lexington as justifiable military acts; but, surely, any theory is more reasonable than that, on the very threshold of a most difficult enterprise, Percy should have been willing to adopt or abet any course of action detrimental to the discipline and control of his troops. If, on the other side of Styx, Percy has been permitted to commune with the shades of Deacon Loring and the Widow Mulliken, I am sure that it required but a few words from him upon military practice, and the nature of his problem, to convince them that the destruction of their property was not wanton, but necessitated by certain grave responsibilities that rested upon him as a soldier.

Active along the line of the Brigade, and busier still in the confusion down by the tavern, are certain young officers with whom generations of American historians have had a long but by no means cordial acquaintance. We are reviewing an old familiar episode of our local history, which for nearly a century and a half has inspired all sorts of publications and all sorts of enthusiasm and oratory. If my version proves out of harmony with generally accepted tradition, it is due in part to
what

what I have learned from these youthful soldiers of
the King. I set small store by a British official report,
and treat it with the same caution that I exercise toward
a provincial affidavit supplied on rush order from the
local Congress at Watertown. But these officers kept
diaries, they wrote good manly letters home, they recorded defeat without peevishness, and their criticism
was directed as much at their own service as at their
foe. They cannot all have known one another; there
is no taint of collusion in what they have to say. I do
not think we can hope to understand what happened
on the road to Charlestown Common if we continue
to slight their evidence merely because we dislike the
uniform they wear.

Lieutenant Mackenzie, of the Royal Welsh Fusileers, seems to have carried a watch on the 19th of
April, and I think that we may, as he did, place some
dependence upon it. At 2 o'clock the Brigade came
within sound of the firing. At 2.30, "being near the
Church at Lexington,"* they formed in line of battle.
At 3.15 the Fusileers, then holding the left of the line,
received orders to form the rear guard. In Mackenzie's
words, "We immediately lined the walls and other
cover in our front with some marksmen, and retired
from the right of Companies by files to the high ground
a small distance in our rear, where we again formed in
line."† Here they remained "for near half an hour,"

* 2 Massachusetts Historical Society *Proceedings* vol. 5, p. 392.
† *Ibid.*, p. 393.

partially

partially hidden doubtless by the smoke screen of the burning houses. It must have been close to four o'clock before they had disappeared down the road beyond the Munroe Tavern, and Earl Percy had made his parting bow to hosts who were glad to have him go.

As we examine the British evidence, it becomes clear that it was not until the arrival of Percy that the officers were conscious of any dominating leadership. Percy, on the other hand, commands unmistakably their confidence and respect. There is no attempt on the part of these officers to minimize the desperate condition of Smith's detachment, and, on the other hand, there is not a shred of evidence to indicate that they felt the slightest anxiety or solicitude for the safety of the column after Percy took command. Washington, on receipt of the first accounts of the action, declared that "if the retreat had not been as precipitate as it was, and God knows it could not well have been more so, the ministerial troops must have surrendered, or been totally cut off";* but we find little trace of any such apprehension in British sources. The British officers had the sort of afternoon that tries men's souls, but I think we may safely conclude that they performed their duties undisturbed by any serious apprehension as to results.†

* May 31, 1775 (*Writings*, ed. Ford, vol. 2, p. 475).

† Percy's report to Gage says: "We arrived at Charlestown, between 7 & 8 in the even, very much fatigued with a march of above 30 miles, & having exhausted almost all our ammunition." (*Letters*, p. 50.) Evidently Percy had ammunition enough, but none to spare. He avoided real peril by following the short route home.

That

That the officers at the tavern did their duty well is evidenced by the fact that by half-past three the Grenadiers and Light Infantry were moving off in the van, followed in order by the 4th and 47th Regiments, the Marines, with the Fusileers covering the rear. Mackenzie states that the Marines relieved the Fusileers as rear guard after seven miles had been covered, and that they in turn were relieved by the other regiments. The American fire was reopened shortly after the march began. Until Menotomy was reached, officers who had served with Smith regarded this fire as light, while in the Brigade it was considered incessant and galling. The flank guards were efficient, and the pressure upon the marching column in the road was materially lessened. Within the area of Menotomy nearly eighteen hundred* fresh minute-men entered the contest, — a force in itself much larger than the effective strength of Percy's command, — and in the long street of the village occurred the heaviest fighting of the day. Here unwary Americans were caught between the flank

---

* As a result of research among the muster-rolls in the Massachusetts Archives, Mr. Frank W. Coburn, of the Lexington Historical Society, estimates the number of provincial reënforcements entering the fight at Arlington as 1779. (*The Battle of April 19, 1775, in Lexington, Concord, etc.*, 1912, p. 135.) Percy, after joining with Smith, had a force of 1500 men, but it is not certain that Smith's men should be rated as effectives on the retreat to Charlestown. Their ammunition was exhausted when they reached Lexington; and, as the Brigade went out with only thirty-six rounds, there could hardly have been any redistribution of powder and ball during the halt. Percy states in his report to Gage that he sent off the Grenadiers and Light Infantry in the van and "covered them" with his Brigade — a hint that these troops may have been more of a hindrance than a help on the retreat. Perhaps such looting as occurred was in large measure due to them.

guards

guards and the marching column, and bayoneted or
clubbed to death. Fierce hand-to-hand fighting occurred within houses, where the bayonets of the British gave them a decided advantage. More than half
the American slain for the day fell along this short two
miles of road. Here Lieutenant-Colonel Bernard, of
the Fusileers, was wounded, and Lieutenant Knight,
of the King's Own, was killed; but when the rear
guard had passed the Menotomy River, the worst of
the fighting was over.*

By this time the flank guards were becoming exhausted; but, on the other hand, the country was more
open and afforded less cover for hostile marksmen.
Percy notes a concentration in force at North Cambridge, which portended a determined attempt to block
his retreat. This formation was broken up by a single
cannon shot, and the action resumed its irregular character. Mackenzie records the presence in the column
of "about ten prisoners, some of whom were taken in
arms. One or two more were killed on the march while
prisoners by the fire of their own people." † Before this,
Percy, suspecting the destruction of the bridge near the
colleges, had determined to follow the short route to

---

* De Bernière (*General Gage's Instructions*, 1779, p. 20; 2 Massachusetts
Historical Society *Collections*, vol. 4, pp. 218–19) gives the casualties among
the officers as two killed and thirteen wounded. Of these, four occurred at the
North Bridge, one near Concord, eight near Lexington, and two in Menotomy.
Probably Lieutenant-Colonel Bernard wounded and Lieutenant Knight killed
in the last-named place were the only officers to fall after Percy began his
march.

† 2 Massachusetts Historical Society *Proceedings*, vol. 5, p. 394.

Charlestown

Charlestown. When he wheeled to the left in North Cambridge, his officers are unanimous in their praise of the move. "We threw them," writes Barker with an enthusiasm foreign to him, "and went on to Charles Town without any great interruption."* Mackenzie records in his diary that Lord Percy "took the resolution of returning by way of Charlestown, which was the shortest road and which could be defended against any number of Rebels."† In a copy of Stedman's *History of the American War*, General Clinton made this manuscript note: "gave them [the Americans] every reason to suppose they would retire by the route they came but fell back on C'Town thus securing his retreat unmolested." Unmolested was too strong a word, but Percy's move was a shrewd one. It took his enemies by surprise, disarranged their plans, and saved both time and lives.

Charlestown had been thrown into a panic by the news that the Cambridge bridge was up, and that the troops were following the road to the Common. Wild rumors of their atrocities were in the air and every one who could get away fled the town. The sun set at half-past six. An hour later the troops were on Bunker Hill, and all firing had ceased. Here they halted while Percy negotiated an agreement with the selectmen, pledging safety to the persons and property of the townsfolk pro-

---

* "Diary of a British Officer in Boston," in *Atlantic Monthly* (1877), vol. 39, p. 400.
† 2 Massachusetts Historical Society *Proceedings*, vol. 5, p. 393.

vided

vided they kept their women within doors, and furnished the soldiers with drink.

By eight o'clock the troops were moving down into the village. Boats from the men-of-war were found waiting at the waterside, and the wounded were placed in them and rowed across to Boston. Returning, they brought General Pigot and a force of five hundred men to occupy the heights commanding the Neck. The Marines and Fusileers were ordered into the Town House while the officers gathered at the tavern hard by. Everywhere the cry was for drink, but there was no hint of riot or disorder. Jacob Rogers, who had fled with his family in the afternoon, came down in the early evening from his refuge at the house of "Mr. Townsend, pump-maker in the training field." Finding all things peaceful, he started back for his wife and sisters, only to meet them coming quietly up the street, escorted by a certain Captain Adams. There is a Pepysian flavor about Rogers's chronicle: "I . . . found an officer and guard under arms by Mr. David Wood's, baker who continued, it seems all night; from thence, seeing everything quiet came home, and went to bed." *

The moon rose shortly after ten and revealed the Somerset man-of war at her old anchorage, where Paul Revere beheld her the night before, and the surface of the harbor dotted with a multitude of slow-moving

* Jacob Rogers's petition, in Frothingham, *History of the Siege of Boston,* p. 372.

boats.

boats. The midnight hour had long since clanged out from Christ Church steeple when the tramp of the war-worn Fusileers returning to their barracks echoed in the silent streets below. Percy was closeted with the Governor at the Province House, and Charlestown after its fitful fever of doubt and terror slept well. I am inclined to think that the behavior of the troops in the little village across the river should be mentioned to Percy's credit as a soldier. He might well have complimented the selectmen on the performance of their part of the agreement, despite that transgression of Mrs. Rogers, her appearance on the street in company with Captain Adams.

That Percy displayed real military ability in his conduct of the retreat from Lexington has never been questioned. Friend and foe found themselves in complete agreement with Lord Drummond's statement to Lord Dartmouth that "a piece of masterly officership" had been performed.* He had brought his fifteen hundred men nearly a dozen miles along an exposed, fire-swept road, standing his enemy off with such success that, according to his own statement, he suffered a loss of only about forty killed.† When we consider the peculiar

---

* June 9, 1775, in Percy's *Letters*, p. 54 note.

† "They kept up a constant fire upon us for upwards of 15 miles, yet only killed of us about 40 men." (Percy to Henry Reveley, May, 1775, in *Letters*, p. 55.) Gage's first report (London *Chronicle*, June 13, 1775, vol. 37, p. 554) gave the British loss for the whole day as 65 killed, 180 wounded, 27 missing, a total of 272. This was subsequently amended (*General Gage's Instructions*, Boston, 1779, p. 20; 2 Massachusetts Historical Society *Collections*, vol. 4, pp. 218–19) to read 73 killed, 174 wounded, 26 missing, a total of 273. Percy's killed during the retreat aggregated a little more than half the fatal casualties for the day.

nature

nature of his problem and that the advantages of numbers, initiative, cover, and choice of ground were always with his adversaries, is it too much to say that he was deserving of all the praise that was lavished upon him in high quarters?

We can hardly dismiss this phase of the subject without some mention of what is known as Percy's baggage-train. American annals teem with details of its progress and fate. It came on far behind the column, with a sergeant's guard of twelve men, and was finally ambushed and captured by a group of armed villagers in Menotomy. Some accounts state that it consisted of two wagons, one loaded with provisions, the other with ammunition. As the legend runs, the guard dispersed upon receiving the provincial fire, which killed two men and several horses. The fugitives fled in the direction of Spy Pond, giving themselves up to old Mother Bathericke, whom they found in a field digging dandelions.* The details of this surrender were transmitted to England, where they stirred caustic comment in the press and on the floor of the House of Commons. Stripped of this dandelion episode, and certain other improbabilities born of local anniversary oratory, the fact remains that the men of Menotomy did lay violent hands upon some portion of His Majesty's property. Strangely enough, there is no mention of the existence or the loss of these supplies in the British official reports, or in the other British evidence upon which we

* Cf. *Colonial Society Publications*, vol. 7, pp. 27–30.

depend.

depend. Mackenzie states that the Brigade went out with a vanguard of fifty men, and a rear guard of as many more, but he says nothing of a train. Had it been officially attached to the column, and gone out in its company as far as the Charles River in Cambridge, surely some of our witnesses should have noted and bewailed its disappearance. We are told that Percy was urged to take out a reserve supply of ball for his six-pounders, but insisted on limiting himself to the capacity of the side boxes. This might be construed as an indication that he had an aversion to baggage on a short forced march. I have wondered whether those mysterious wagons could have been an after-thought of the headquarters in Boston. Gage made up his mind slowly, and his best-laid plans were wont to miscarry.*

We now come to the consideration of the charges of vandalism and brutality that have been brought against Percy, and I will ask you to listen to the indictments. This is from the first account sent to England by the provincial authorities: "They pillaged almost every House they passed by, breaking and de-

---

* The Reverend Dr. David McClure, writing April 19, 1775, seems in a measure to support this theory: " A waggon loaded with provisions was sent from Boston, for the refreshment of the retreating army, under an escort of 6 Granidiers. They got as far as this place, [Menotomy], when a number of men, 10 or 12, collected, and ordered them to surrender. They marched on, & our men fired, killed the driver & the horses, when the rest fled a little way, & surrendered. Another waggon sent on the same business, was also taken that day. It was strange that General Gage should send them through a country, in which he had just kindled the flames of war, in so defenceless a condition." (*Diary*, ed. F. B. Dexter, 1899, p. 161; cf. 1 Massachusetts Historical Society *Proceedings*, vol. 16, p. 158.)

stroying

stroying Doors, Windows, Glasses, etc. and carrying off Cloathing and other valuable Effects. It appeared to be their Design to burn and destroy all before them; and nothing but our vigorous Pursuit prevented their infernal Purposes from being put in Execution. But the savage Barbarity exercised upon the Bodies of our unfortunate Brethren who fell, is almost incredible: Not content with shooting down the unarmed, aged and infirm, they disregarded the Cries of the wounded, killing them without Mercy, and mangling their Bodies in the Most shocking Manner."*

Here is an extract from the sermon of the Reverend Dr. Samuel Langdon, President of Harvard College, preached before the Congress at Watertown on May 31, 1775: "They acted the part of Robbers and Savages, by burning, plundering and damaging almost every house in their way, to the utmost of their power, murdering the unarmed and helpless, and not regarding the weakness of the tender sex, until they had secured themselves beyond the reach of our terrifying arms." †

Hear what the Reverend Jonas Clark has to say, in a sermon preached at Lexington, April 19, 1776: "After they were joined by *Piercy's brigade*, in Lexington, it seemed as if *all the little remains* of humanity

* *Essex Gazette*, April 25, 1775, p. 3/2–3. Also printed in the *Massachusetts Spy* of May 3, 1775, p. 3/2; and reprinted in Almon's *Remembrancer*, 1775, vol. 1, p. 33; *Force*, vol. 2, p. 439, etc.

† "Government corrupted by Vice, and recovered by Righteousness. A Sermon," etc. (Watertown, 1775), p. 8.

had

had left them; and rage and revenge had taken the reins, and knew no bounds! *Cloathing, furniture, provisions, goods, plundered, carried off, or destroyed! Buildings (especially dwelling houses) abused, defaced, battered, shattered and almost ruined! And as if this had not been enough, numbers of them doomed to the flames! . . . Add to all this; the unarmed, the aged and infirm, who were unable to flee, are inhumanly stabbed and murdered in their habitations! Yea, even women in child-bed, with their helpless babes in their arms, do not escape the horrid alternative, of being either cruelly murdered in their beds, burnt in their habitations, or turned into the streets to perish with cold, nakedness and distress! But I forbear — words are too insignificant to express, the horrid barbarities of that distressing day!"*

In the middle of the nineteenth century, Bancroft and Frothingham reflected these accusations in a fashion that would have satisfied the earliest prosecutors; and in 1880 the Reverend Charles Hudson, the historian of Lexington, declared before the Massachusetts Historical Society "that we have discovered no general traces of barbarity until the troops became subject to Percy's command, when a general system of vandalism prevailed."† Since then it has been customary to depict the British commander as devising and practising a brutal method of warfare abhorrent to civ-

---

* *Narrative*, pp. 7–8, appended to his "Fate of Blood-thirsty Oppressors, and God's tender Care of his distressed People. A Sermon," etc., Boston, 1776.

† 1 Massachusetts Historical Society *Proceedings*, vol. 17, p. 322.

ilized

ilized standards. He is held personally responsible for some half-dozen alleged offences of the troops against non-combatants, all that in nearly a century and a half it has been possible to unearth.

Before reviewing specific acts, let us consider the broad charge of vandalism and brutality. I will at the outset submit the evidence of some of the King's officers whose qualifications as witnesses I have already explained.

They "concealed themselves in *houses*, & advanced within 10 yds. to fire at me & other officers," writes Percy, in discussing the provincial morale in a private letter to General Harvey.*

"The soldiers shewed great bravery . . . forceing *houses* from whence came a heavy fire." This is the entry of Ensign Henry de Bernière, of the 10th Regiment, in his diary found in Boston after the withdrawal of the British garrison.†

Captain W. Glanville Evelyn, of the King's Own, writes to his reverend father in Ireland: "We observed on our march [out] . . . that the *houses* along the road were all shut up as if deserted, though we afterwards found these *houses* full of men, and only forsaken by the women and children; having executed our orders, and being on our return to Boston, we were attacked on all

---

* April 20, 1775, in *Letters*, p. 53. The italics in the extracts which immediately follow are mine.

† *General Gage's Instructions, Of 22d February 1775, . . . With a curious Narrative. . . . Also an Account*, etc., Boston, 1779, p. 19. Cf. 2 Massachusetts Historical Society *Collections*, vol. 4, p. 218.

sides

sides, from woods and orchards, and stone walls, and from every *house* on the roadside (and this country is a continued village), so that for fourteen miles we were attacking fresh posts, and under one incessant fire. . . . Whenever we were fired on from *houses* or *barns*, our men dashed in, and let very few of those they could find escape." *

Here is what Mackenzie of the Fusileers has to say: "Before the Column had advanced a mile on the road, we were fired on from all quarters, but particularly from the *houses* on the roadside & the adjacent stone walls. . . . The soldiers were so enraged at suffering from an unseen enemy, that they forced open many of the *houses* from which the fire proceeded & put to death all those found in them. These *houses* would certainly have been burnt had any fire been found in them, or had there been time to kindle any, . . . Some *houses* were forced open in which no person could be discovered, but when the Column had passed, numbers sallied out from some place in which they had lain concealed, fired at the rear Guard, and augmented the numbers which followed us. If we had had time to set fire to these *houses* many Rebels must have perished in them, . . . Many *houses* were plundered by the soldiers, notwithstanding the efforts of the officers to prevent it. I have no doubt this influenced the Rebels, & many of them followed us further than they would other-

* April 23, 1775, in *Memoir and Letters* (ed. G. D. Scull, Oxford, 1879), p. 54.

wise

wise have done. By all accounts some soldiers who stayed too long in the *houses* were killed in the very act of plundering by those that lay concealed in them."*

And now comes Barker, of the King's Own, that testy young subaltern of a keenly critical mind. In his diary you read as follows: "We set out upon our return; before the whole had quitted the Town we were fired on from *Houses* and behind Trees, and before we had gone ½ a mile we were fired on from all sides, but mostly from the Rear, where people had hid themselves in *houses* till we had passed, and then fired; . . . We were now obliged to force almost every *house* in the road, for the Rebels had taken possession of them and galled us exceedingly; but they suffered for their temerity, for all that were found in the *houses* were put to death. . . .† Our Soldiers the other day, tho' they shew'd no want of courage, yet were so wild and irregular, that there was no keeping 'em in any order; by their eagerness and inattention they killed many of our own People, and the plundering was shameful; many hardly thought of anything else; what was worse they were encouraged by some Officers."‡

Lieutenant-Colonel

* 2 Massachusetts Historical Society *Proceedings*, vol. 5, pp. 393, 394.
† April 19, 1775; in *Atlantic Monthly*, vol. 39, p. 400.
‡ April 23, 1775, in *Atlantic Monthly*, vol. 39, p. 544. Confirmation of the character of the fighting is found in intercepted letters of British private soldiers printed in *Force*. One man writes, April 28: "They did not fight us like a regular army, only like savages, behind trees and stone walls, and out of the woods and houses, where in the latter we killed numbers of them." (4 *American Archives*, vol. 2, p. 440.) Another writes, April 28: "When we found they fired from the houses, we set them on fire, and they ran to the woods like

Lieutenant-Colonel James Abercrombie, of the 22d Regiment, did not arrive in Boston until the 23d of April, or four days after the battle. On May 2, after making "the Strictest enquiry amongst the Officers," he penned his analysis of the event to his friend Lieutenant-Governor Colden of New York: "They were fired on from every *House* and fense along the Road for fifteen Miles. I cannot commend the behavior of Our Soldiers on the retreat. As they began to plunder, & payed no obediance to their Officers."*

Here is a body of evidence coming from a variety of sources, all unofficial in its character, and indicating in unmistakable terms that the fighting throughout the afternoon was of the house-to-house variety. The British and American accounts agree on the use of trees, walls, orchards, and other cover; but the early American witnesses are wholly silent as to the firing from houses. Read what Holmes has to say in his *American Annals:* "An irregular yet very galling fire was kept up on each flank, as well as in the front and rear. The close firing from behind *stone walls* by good marksmen put them in no small confusion."† Or turn to Thacher's *Military Journal* and read the following: "The provincials concealed themselves behind *stone walls,*

like devils." (*Ibid.*, p. 440.) A soldier of the Royal Welsh Fusileers in addressing his "Dear Parents," April 30, records the following: "As we came along they got before us and fired at us out of the houses, and killed and wounded a great number of us, but we levelled their houses, as we came along." (*Ibid.*, p. 440.)

* 2 Massachusetts Historical Society *Proceedings*, vol. 11, p. 306.
† *American Annals* (1805), vol. 2, p. 327; (1829) vol. 2, p. 206.

and

and with a sure aim thinned the enemies' ranks."* You find the same note in Gordon's *History:* "The close firing from behind the *walls,* by good marksmen, . . . put the troops into no small confusion."†

Why this prominence given to houses on the one side and to stone walls on the other? Were our British friends deceived, were they all lying as they wrote their diaries and addressed their relatives and friends, or were our ancestors writing history in ignorance of facts or with an exaggerated sense of duty to their cause? There is something to be said in support of the theory of ignorance. It is doubtful whether any one person, acting with the uncommanded thousands that sustained the popular cause that day, could have known to what extent houses were being used as a menace to the troops. The men who fought the British in Menotomy and Cambridge were strangers in those towns; they came from long distances, and included two or three companies of Pickering's regiment from Essex County. They ranged about at will, in small groups, and all windows appealed to them as convenient loopholes from which to shoot a redcoat. The American contention has been from the first that the damage inflicted by the troops on private property was unprovoked and wanton; and upon this premise rest all the charges alleging against Percy ruthlessness and worse. Mr. Hudson admitted in 1880 that the British were justified in

---

* *Military Journal during the American Revolution* (1823), p. 19.
† *History* (1788), vol. 1, p. 482.

attacking

attacking any house from which they were fired upon.*
To my mind it is clear beyond all reasonable doubt
that the fighting along Percy's line of march was of
the kind so minutely described by Abercrombie and
his comrades. Tons of depositions turned off on provincial presses to meet the political exigencies of the
hour cannot break the force of such evidence as this.

When the Provincials drifted into the practice of
using private houses as fortresses, they certainly adopted
the best military policy to retard and demoralize their
foe. By so doing they also placed all such private property under suspicion and in actual jeopardy. Their tactics introduced new problems for the British, and went
far to nullify the control of battalion and company officers. As the aim of the Provincials was to impede,
wear down, and ultimately capture their foe, so the
purpose of the British was merely to cover their distance before the setting of the sun. The movement of
the column continued steadily eastward at the rate of
about three miles an hour, but the constant detailing
of squads to clean up belligerent posts must have re-
sulted in the hopeless mixing of units and the serious
impairment of discipline. It was a difficult business to
keep track of the groups operating indoors and to get
them out before the rear guard came along. Is it rea-

* "We do not censure him [Percy] for any warlike attacks upon our
troops, or for firing upon any dwelling within which our soldiers had taken
refuge, or from which they assailed the king's troops. So far he would be
justified by the laws of war." 1 Massachusetts Historical Society *Proceedings*, vol. 17, p. 322.

sonable

sonable to suppose that anything but the most imperative military necessity would have tempted the officers
to engage their men in indoor fighting, conscious as
they were of the long miles ahead and of the wester-
ing sun sinking surely to its rest? There were bad men
in Percy's rank and file, and plenty of light-fingered
gentry, as there were in Washington's army in Cambridge a few weeks later. And so, in the words of Abercrombie, "they began to plunder."

We find nothing in the official reports of Gage or
Percy concerning the misdemeanors of the troops, and
it is well that we can mingle with our youthful witnesses and hear from them the frank gossip of the messroom. And yet it is possible that we may take their
confessions too seriously. The British officer of that
day, however easy-going in his personal habits, was a
martinet in the performance of his professional duty.
He had been taught the old-time military maxim, that
an army that plunders is never a good one. To him,
looting was a loathsome thing because it begot straggling and insubordination and was in every way sub-
versive of discipline. We cannot accept our British
evidence as confirming the American assertion that
Percy's men staggered along the Boston road under a
weight of ill-gotten plunder. Looting of some sort was
certain to accompany the mode of fighting the British
had had forced upon them. But, despite Barker's caustic thrust at some one, the officers were evidently vigi-
lant, the column was cumbered with the transportation
of

of wounded, the flank guards required frequent relief, skirmishing was incessant, there was a heavy pressure on the rear guard, and altogether there was too much to do, and too little time to allow of getting away with substantial plunder. Small articles for which the knapsack was a convenient receptacle did suffer, food and drink for obvious reasons were swept away, but on the whole I fear that, from the standpoint of an ambitious looter, the day's work was not altogether a happy one.

Now looting begets straggling, or is the result of it. If you will turn to the British official report—and there are times in reading American history when official reports as well as affidavits must be consulted — you will find the total British missing for the day given as 26.* A score of these we can trace from provincial sources to the captured baggage-train, and to the period of Smith's command before Percy had arrived upon the scene. Is it reasonable to suppose that a force of fifteen hundred men could have marched under fire twelve miles through an enemy's country, systematically plundering all the way, and have appeared at roll-call the next morning with only six men missing? The officers were shamed by the wildness, inattention, and disobedience that cropped up among their men; and yet, as you read and re-read the story of the march, you are impressed with the fact that on the whole they dominated a difficult situation, and did their duty well.

And then the thought occurs, what wretched prop-

* Cf. p. 99, note †, above.

agandists

agandists these martial Britons were! The whole coun-
tryside was accusing them as destroyers and plunderers
of private property, and, conscious of a measure of
guilt, they remained silent and inert. Had they possessed a fraction of the political sagacity displayed by
their foes, they might have set up a very plausible defence. Abercrombie had his chance. Might he not have
urged in all sincerity that the British were not the first
or the last strangers to infest deserted houses on the 19th
of April, and that the charge of exclusive opportunity
could not be levelled against the troops? Was it not
true that, for every minute allowed a soldier in which
to misbehave, scores of light-fingered Provincials had
an hour? But his mind could not shape itself to prop-
aganda. He had no interest in the exaggerations or
possible misdeeds of his enemy. His Majesty's troops
had misbehaved, they had begun to plunder, and as an
honest officer he was disgusted and sick at heart.*

Of course, vandalism is an evil of which looting is
but a single phase. Houses along the road were battered and shattered in battle, and other minor damage
was doubtless wrought in wantonness and hate. I think
that in any Boston messroom on the 20th of April we

* Gage's defence, written to Governor Trumbull May 3, 1775, is as follows: "The troops disclaim with indignation the barbarous outrages of which
they are accused, so contrary to their known humanity. I have taken the
greatest pains to discover if any were committed, and have found examples
of their tenderness, both to the young and the old, but no vestige of cruelty
or barbarity. It is very possible that in firing into houses, from whence
they were fired upon, old people, women, or children may have suffered,
but if any such thing has happened, it was in their defence and undesigned."
(*Trumbull Papers*, vol. 2, pp. 298-99.)

should

should have received frank admissions from the officers that probably some houses were entered by mistake, and that possibly others known to be innocent were invaded by small groups, temporarily out of hand. It is certain that the soldier was in an ugly mood. He had gone out despising the Boston mob, and his temper had not been improved by his experiences on the road. If opportunity offered to drive his bayonet through a mirror or to break china in the corner cupboard, many a man there was who would have regarded the occasion as Heaven-sent.

Mackenzie is the only one of the officers we have cited who alludes to the burning of houses. Our gallant Fusileer writes in shame and humiliation of the looting, but he records incendiarism as merely a necessary and ordinary episode of the day. If we admit the contention of the British that the fighting was of the house-to-house character, their disposition to keep the home fires burning falls into the category of a mere commonplace of war. This accounts for omission to mention it in the diaries and letters of our other witnesses. All incendiarism, except that practised during the halt in Lexington, proved abortive, owing to the closeness with which the Provincials followed the rear guard, a fact that Mackenzie records with evident regret.

The earliest provincial account alleged that the British disregarded the appeals of the wounded, killing and mangling without mercy. Now the Provincials' killed exceeded the number of their wounded, a fact that in

some

some measure confirms the charge;* but we must remember that, aside from those slain by gun-fire at Lexington and at the North Bridge, nearly all the Provincials killed fell in close combat within houses or in hastily constructed defences outside. We have just noted the temper of the private soldier. He had been fooled, ambushed, and shot in the back, until he had lost all faith in American non-combatants, and was strongly of the opinion that the only good American was a dead one. On the other hand, the hatred of the people for the troops, always fanatical in its intensity, had become inflamed by what they regarded as the unprovoked slaughter at Lexington and Concord. I doubt that quarter was asked, or thought of, in those fierce hand-to-hand fights along Percy's line of march, and the bayonet and gunstock did make ugly wounds.

We come now to the consideration of specific outrages inflicted by the troops upon the persons of inoffensive non-combatants. There are just six cases of this sort that call for examination. Three of them fall naturally into one group: the killing of John Raymond at the Munroe Tavern in Lexington; of William Marcy in North Cambridge; and of the fourteen-year-old lad Barber on Charlestown Neck.

Raymond's name appeared on the first lists of the Provincial slain, but it was not until fifty years later that he took his place in history as the victim of a mili-

* The provincial losses are given by Phinney (*History of the Battle of Lexington*, 1825, pp. 27–30) as 49 killed, 36 wounded, 5 missing, a total of 90.

tary

tary outrage. William Munroe, the proprietor of the tavern, who was out with the minute-men on the 19th of April, made the following deposition in 1825: "On the return of the British troops from Concord, they stopped at my tavern house in Lexington, and dressed their wounded. I had left my house in the care of a lame man, by the name of Raymond, who supplied them with whatever the house afforded, and afterward, when he was leaving the house, he was shot by the regulars, and found dead within a few rods of the house." *
This brief statement of Munroe's suggests an atrocity, and a tradition, plausible but none too robust, has developed since 1825, to the effect that Raymond, after mixing a punch, left the place in fear of his life and was shot by soldiers as he was hobbling away. The setting for this tragic legend was well chosen if you agree with me that there was probably trouble and disorder within the tavern, where maddened men of Smith's detachment came thronging and panting to the bar. Credible as the story is, it has never become solidly established in the annals of the day. Both Frothingham and Bancroft ignored it, and we might well follow their example had not Hudson revitalized the tale in his *History of Lexington* † and in a contribution to Drake's *History of Middlesex County*. Here are his words, taken from the last-named work: "The officers with Percy resorted to Munroe's tavern just below. The occupants

---

* In Phinney's Appendix to *History of the Battle of Lexington* (1825), pp. 34-35.

† (1868), p. 202; (1913), vol. i, p. 175.

of the house left the place in affright, leaving only John Raymond, an aged man, who was at the time one of the family. The intruders ordered him to supply them with all the good things the house afforded, which he readily did. But after they had imbibed too freely, they became noisy, and so alarmed Raymond that he sought to escape from the house; but was brutally fired upon and killed in his attempt to flee from danger." *

The credibility of Munroe's story has not been enhanced by this elaboration of Hudson. I think that I have proved beyond any reasonable doubt that the soldiers about the tavern were of Smith's command, and that the Brigade in battle formation, nearly half a mile away, was involved in skirmishing throughout the halt. It is clear also that, inasmuch as it was close to half-past two when Smith came within sight of the Brigade, and at half-past three his men resumed their march down the Boston road, their presence in and about the tavern could not have consumed much more than half an hour.† Hudson's tale of Percy's carousal with his officers suggests poetical or historical license, and may have been responsible for the christening of the tavern as "Earl Percy's Headquarters."

I have tried to show what Percy's problems and responsibilities were at Lexington, and I think you will

---

* *History of Middlesex County* (1880), vol. 2, p. 26.

† This agrees with De Bernière's estimate, "The whole halted for about half an hour to rest." (*General Gage's Instructions, 1779*, p. 19; 2 Massachusetts Historical Society *Collections*, vol. 4, p. 218.)

agree

agree with me that, if he galloped down the road once or twice for a momentary inspection of what Pitcairn* was doing, this was about all the time or attention he could have allowed to the vicinity of Munroe's Tavern. Had the officers of the Grenadiers and Light Infantry spent their precious time in the diversions portrayed by Hudson, drinking themselves into a state of noisy exaltation, the Fusileers would hardly have received their orders to form the rear guard at 3.15, and the van would have been fortunate to have passed over Charlestown Common by the light of the rising moon.

Now Munroe, an honest man, deposing at eighty-two years of age concerning events that happened fifty years before, states that Raymond was lame; Hudson, in every way a worthy and distinguished citizen, declared that he was oppressed by the burden of years.† If you will turn to the genealogical register appended to Hudson's history ‡ of the town, capably edited and

* Placing Pitcairn in command of the troops near Munroe's Tavern is a mere conjecture, as his name is not mentioned by any of our witnesses after Percy took command. Possibly Bernard was in command at this point, and Pitcairn may have been assigned to the Marine battalion that came out with the Brigade. Whoever commanded the Marines seems to have borne the brunt of the afternoon's fighting. If we estimate the strength of the battalion at four or five companies, or not more than 175 men, we cannot be far from the truth. Two other companies may have gone out with Smith. The official report, giving the total regimental losses in killed and wounded, indicates that 27 per cent of the casualties were suffered by the Marines. If we confine ourselves to the killed, the Marine percentage was 37. This is an extraordinary showing when compared with the 14 per cent of the King's Own Regiment, the next heaviest sufferer. These figures suggest that nearly 50 per cent of Percy's casualties on the retreat occurred in the Marines.

† In 1880: see p. 280, note 3. In 1868 Hudson had merely called him "infirm." (*History of Lexington*, p. 202; *Genealogical Register*, p. 189.)

‡ (1913), vol. 2, p. 552. Cf. Lexington Vital Records, p. 62.

handsomely

handsomely republished by the Lexington Historical Society, you will find that John Raymond was born September 5, 1731, and so was in his forty-fourth year at the time of his death. Moreover, you will learn here and from other sources that he was a regularly enlisted member of Captain Parker's company, from which fact we might well infer that the lameness mentioned by Munroe was merely a temporary affliction. He was one of the numerous absentees from the early morning muster on the Common, and we cannot trace his movements between that time and his appearance at the tavern in the afternoon. Of course, if the British had learned, or if they suspected, his military status, they would have treated him as a prisoner; and if as a prisoner he tried to escape, he would very probably have been shot. Fifty years was a long time to wait for Raymond's conversion from the status of an apparent belligerent to the category of an aged and infirm victim of British brutality. I find it hard to resist the conviction that, had murder been committed at the tavern, as alleged by Mr. Hudson in 1880, Langdon and Clark would have exploited the fact in 1775. Clark's silence is the more remarkable because the tragedy occurred within the narrow limits of the parish that had been confided to his spiritual charge.*

The first mention of Marcy's fate is to be found in

* We have quoted Mackenzie as saying, that one or two Provincials "were killed on the march while prisoners by the fire of their own people." Is it possible that Raymond was taken from Munroe's Tavern as a prisoner, and killed by an American bullet before or as soon as the march began?

the

the sermon preached by President Langdon before the Congress of the Colony, May 31, 1775: "A man of weak mental powers, who went out to gaze at the regular army as they pass'd, without arms, or thought of danger, was wantonly shot at and kill'd by those inhuman butchers, as he sat on a fence."* If we accept this statement at its face value, we may yet question the wanton character of the deed. Perhaps more than one soldier who had been straining his eyes for a fair shot at some of the hidden marksmen who were picking off his comrades saw, through drifting powder-smoke, Marcy seated on the fence. I think we may assume that his slayer knew nothing of his mental deficiencies, or suspected that he was unarmed. If the fall of the victim was noticed in the column, I am afraid that the sentiment aroused was not one of pity, but of grim satisfaction that one enemy had received his just deserts.

We have an interesting side-light on this case that is somewhat harmful to Langdon's hasty conjecture. Near the present corner of Massachusetts Avenue and Spruce Street in North Cambridge, a party of Provincials had taken position behind a barricade of empty casks. They fell victims to the vigilance of a flank guard, a hot fight ensued, and Isaac Gardner, Esq., of Brookline, John Hicks and Moses Richardson, of Cambridge, and one or two others, were killed. We have it on the authority of the Widow Hicks that, alarmed

* Sermon, p. 9, note.

by

by the long absence of her husband from home, she in the early evening sent her fourteen-year-old son in search of him. The boy found him lying by the roadside, dead, and near him were the bodies of Moses Richardson and William Marcy. This places Marcy in the midst of undoubted combatants, on the very spot where one of the sharpest encounters of the day occurred; and we know that he was buried with Richardson and Hicks in a common grave on the night of the battle.* In view of these facts, we must regard Langdon's statement with serious misgiving. All that we know of William Marcy himself is contained in the following extract from the records of the Cambridge selectmen, dated September 3, 1770: "Voted, to warn out of the town, William Marcy, a man of very poor circumstances; he for some time hath lodged in Steward Hastings' barn, the Steward paying the charges."† Marcy made a more dignified exit from Cambridge than the selectmen had planned, and his name is now inscribed on a monument erected by the city in 1870 to commemorate "the Men of Cambridge who fell in defence of the Liberty of the People, April 19, 1775."

Barber was the youthful brother-in-law of Rogers, whom we met in Charlestown, from whose affidavit we learn that the lad was shot as he was looking out from a window on Charlestown Neck. Curiously enough, Mackenzie mentions these houses "close to the Neck,

* Paige, *History of Cambridge*, p. 413.   † *Ibid.*, p. 413, note.

out

out of which the Rebels fired to the last."* It was a pity that, at a time when so many were fleeing for their lives, this boy should have been left gazing from a window among houses from which firing was still going on. The sun had set when the British passed this point. In the gloaming the lad's youth and innocence were not discernible to the soldiers, but the sight of a face in the window had come to have a sinister significance to them. So Barber went down to his death, but not, I think, as the victim of a military atrocity.

The fourth case is that concerning Hannah, wife of Deacon Joseph Adams, of Menotomy. She made affidavit to the facts on May 17, 1775. Two weeks later, President Langdon epitomized the case in the following words: "A woman in bed with a new-born infant, about a week old, was forced by the threats of the soldiery, to escape, almost naked, to an open outhouse; her house was then set on fire, but soon extinguished by one of the children which had laid concealed till the enemy was gone." † This was the incident that inspired that passionate outburst of the Reverend Jonas Clark: "Yea, even women in child-bed with their helpless babes in their arms, do not escape the horrid alternative, of being either cruelly murdered in their beds, burned in their habitations, or turned into the streets to perish with cold and nakedness and distress!"‡

* 2 Massachusetts Historical Society *Proceedings*, vol. 5, p. 394.
† Sermon, pp. 8–9, notes.   ‡ Cf. p. 103, above.

Hannah

Hannah Adams states* that, as she lay in her bed, three soldiers broke into her room. As one pointed his bayonet at her breast, she cried out in terror, " For the Lord's sake, do not kill me!" There was little comfort in the profane and laconic reply of, "Damn you!" Here a comrade interposed with the words, "We will not hurt the woman, if she will go out of the house, but we will surely burn it." Leaving in the house "five children and no other person," she threw a blanket about her and with her babe "crawled into a corn-house near the door," but fortunately not "to perish with cold, nakedness and distress" on that bright April afternoon.

This is not a pleasant story, but perhaps it hardly justifies the fevered denunciation of the Reverend Jonas Clark. It is notable as the one recorded instance of indignity offered by the soldiery to the gentler sex. Here in this room, so far as the 19th of April is concerned, we see the British soldier at his worst. The stage was set in every detail for a most revolting tragedy, rude and angry soldiers and an unprotected mother with her children. But the villains in the piece were not of the deepest dye, there was no lust for butchery in their hearts, nor had they a mind that Mrs. Adams should be burned alive in her habitation. What the three uniformed offenders would have said in their own defence we shall never know. Were they part of a squad acting

* May 16, 1775, in *Journals of the Massachusetts Provincial Congress* (1838), p. 677.

under

under orders to burn the place, or were they stragglers? It is certain that no officer was with them. It would be interesting to know a little more of the attendant circumstances, and whether it were possible that, as Mrs. Adams lay in her room, some part of the premises had been put to military uses by armed Patriots from out of town. If the house had been so used, or if the soldiers believed such to be the fact, they would, of course, have regarded Mrs. Adams with some suspicion, and might even have been inclined to question the age of her babe. We cannot summon Deacon Adams as a witness, because he ran away and was throughout the episode lying concealed under hay in the barn of the Reverend Samuel Cooke.* The soldiers had seen him leave the house, and he had drawn their fire in his flight across the fields. Possibly this precautionary measure of his may account in part for the military invasion of his home.†

Now Hannah Adams's infant was eighteen days old

---

* Samuel Cooke (1708–1783; H. C. 1735) was long the minister of the Second Precinct, Cambridge (now Arlington).

† In 1864, the Reverend Samuel A. Smith gave us this account of Deacon Adams's activities. He "knew that his life would be in danger, both on account of his name, and also for his reputation for patriotic zeal, but thinking that they would not harm women and children, as the troops came in sight left his house, . . . and fled across the fields. He was hotly pursued, and, as he was running under cover of the stone walls, he heard the bullets whistle over his head. He kept on, however, and had just time to cover himself over in the hay-loft in Reverend Mr. Cooke's barn, . . . when his pursuers came up and began to search for him, sticking their bayonets here and there into the hay. They did not dare to remain long, and he escaped." (*West Cambridge on the Nineteenth of April, 1775*, p. 34.)

Deacon Adams was a prominent man in the community, was precinct treasurer for nineteen years and selectman of Cambridge for four years.

on

on the 19th of April.* This child grew into woman-
hood, married, and must often have heard her mother,
who lived until 1803, discuss with the older children
the family experiences in which they were participants
on that fateful day. We might well expect that the
terrors of the episode would increase with repeated
telling, but, on the contrary, under the mild influence
of the family tradition, the Reverend Jonas Clark's
denunciation has long since lost its force. We are
told that Mrs. Adams was fully dressed on the arrival of the soldiers, having been assisted in that proc-
ess by two daughters aged respectively twenty and fourteen. The brutal redcoats degenerate into mere bur-
glars of a rather genial type. "Why don't you come
out here?" queries a soldier, when the head of nine-
year-old Joel Adams is thrust from under a bed.
"You'll kill me if I do," replies the prudent boy. "No,
we won't," is the prompt and reassuring reply. Then
out crawls the child and follows the soldiers about, a
rapt spectator of their activities, which are largely of
a pilfering nature. We are told that, when they laid
thieving hands upon the church communion silver,
Joel ventured a word of warning and an assurance that
the deacon would "lick" them for that offence.† A

* Born April 1, 1775. Her name is given as Ann by Paige (*History of
Cambridge*, p. 478), as Ann or Anne by Cutter (*History of Arlington*, pp.
185, 260), but as Anna in Cambridge Vital Records, vol. 2, p. 10. She
married James Hill (1773–1852) on October 11, 1796. In 1831, Hannah
Hill, daughter of James and Ann (Adams) Hill, married Thomas Hall.

† This is the story as repeated in 1854 by Mrs. Hill, then in her eightieth
year, to Samuel Griffin Damon; see *Christian Register*, October 28, 1854,
vol. 39, p. 169.

touch

touch of the original tragic flavor is restored to the story, when, upon leaving, the soldiers break up the chairs and set them alight with a brand from the fireplace. Then comedy once more gaily trips the stage in the person of the youthful Joel, who saves the situation by attacking the flames with a pot of the deacon's home-brewed beer.*

In the next case we have to consider, the authorities began to disagree at the outset. President Langdon states that "two aged helpless men who had not been out in the action, and were found unarmed in a house where the Regulars enter'd, were murdered without mercy." † After a year of reflection the Reverend Mr. Clark referred to the incident in these words, "the unarmed, the aged and infirm, who were unable to flee, are inhumanly stabbed and murdered in their habitations!" ‡ Between the dates of these statements of Langdon and Clark, the tragedy had been located, not in the habitations of the victims, but in the bar-room of the Cooper Tavern in Menotomy. Here is an extract from the deposition of Landlord Benjamin Cooper and his wife, Rachel, dated May 19, 1775: "The king's regular troops . . . fired more than a hundred bullets into the house where we dwelt, through doors, windows, &c. Then a number of them entered the house, where we and two aged gentlemen were all unarmed. We escaped for our lives into the cellar. The

---

* S. A. Smith, *West Cambridge on the Nineteenth of April, 1775*, p. 37.
† Sermon, p. 8 note.   ‡ See p. 103, above.

two

two aged gentlemen were, immediately, most barbarously and inhumanly murdered by them: being
stabbed through in many places, their heads mauled,
skulls broken, and their brains dashed out on the floor
and walls of the house."* Now these two aged men
were Jason Winship and Jabez Wyman. and we learn
from the genealogical records of Cambridge and Woburn that they were brothers-in-law, aged respectively
forty-five and thirty-nine years.† We learn, too, from a
letter of that stanch Patriot, the Reverend John Marrett,
of Woburn, dated July 28, 1775, that "they were drinking flip"; and, in utter disagreement with the views of
the Reverend Jonas Clark, that they "both died like
fools." He was "not certain they were unarmed," but on
making inquiry was informed that such was the fact.‡

Our local historians in accepting the story of the flip
are far from admitting that "both died like fools."
To my mind the second fact is a necessary corollary of
the first, and they must stand or fall together. We must

* May 19, 1775, in *Journals of the Massachusetts Provincial Congress*,
p. 678.

† Jason Winship was baptized in Cambridge June 28, 1730 (Paige, *History of Cambridge*, p. 697). Jabez Wyman was baptized in Woburn December 26, 1736 (Bond, *Genealogies and History of Watertown*, vol. 2, p.
976). (The statement in Paige's *History of Cambridge*, p. 412, that Wyman
was born July 24, 1710, is clearly an error.) Wyman married Lydia Winship (sister of Jason) in Cambridge January 13, 1767 (Cambridge Vital
Records, vol. 2, p. 437). On March 23, 1773, Jabez Wyman, of Cambridge, "laborer," and wife Lydia, deeded land in Arlington to Ammi Cutter.
The Reverend John Marrett states (in *S. Dunster, Henry Dunster and his Descendants*, 1876, p. 88) that Wyman at one time worked for the Reverend
Mr. Cooke.

‡ In *S. Dunster, Henry Dunster and his Descendants*, pp. 88, 89. The
letter was written by Marrett to his uncle the Reverend Isaiah Dunster.

remember

remember that, at the very moment these aged and unarmed men were engaged in their legitimate and private business, there was raging all along the half-mile of road to the west the heaviest fighting of the day. Hundreds of newly arrived Americans trained their muskets upon the redcoats; gunstocks thundered on the surface of splintering doors; and all along the village street the British gun-fire rattled and rolled. Old Samuel Whittemore, seventy-nine years of age, went clanking by the tavern door with his newly cleaned musket and pistols, and a newly ground edge upon his sword. He concealed himself at a point but a few hundred feet distant from where Landlord Cooper stood at his bar, and opened fire as the British vanguard came along. He was discovered after killing his man. From the road and from the rear there was a rush upon him. It is alleged that two more Britons fell before a bullet from the flank guard entered his head. Wounded and helpless upon the ground, he was savagely clubbed and bayoneted by the infuriated soldiery. Sturdy efforts have been made to include this affair in the list of Percy's barbarities, notwithstanding the fact that the old gentleman made a happy and complete recovery, dying finally at the ripe age of ninety-seven, leaving, we are told, a virile progeny of one hundred and eighty-five souls.*

* *Columbian Centinel*, February 6, 1793, p. 3/2. For further information concerning Samuel Whittemore, see S. A. Smith, *West Cambridge on the Nineteenth of April, 1775*, pp. 42-44; Cutter, *History of Arlington*, pp. 75-77, 317; Paige, *History of Cambridge*, pp. 414-15, 688.

Must

Must we believe that, in this perturbed environment, Benjamin Cooper and his wife Rachel, Winship, and Wyman, did play their unconcerned and stolid parts at the tavern bar, as has been long alleged? Can we doubt that a fire, or a runaway horse in Menotomy Street on the day before, would have thrown all four into a fever of excitement, and a whirlwind of motion? The quaffing of flip was not the opportunity of a lifetime; prohibition had not then been born. Yet there they stand at the bar as those hundred bullets come whistling through the place, and the soldiers come roaring and cursing into the room. The landlord and his wife vanish away, but the two victims stand their ground until such brains as the legend leaves in their possession are beaten out and spattered upon the walls.

It is reasonably clear that the Reverend John Marrett believed the victims at the Cooper Tavern to have been drunk; and, if we accept this theory, it goes far to explain an otherwise incomprehensible incident. Marrett speaks plainly, as witness these words: "They were drinking flip. Wyman was warned of the danger but says he, 'let us finish the mug, they won't come yet.' He died as a fool dieth." If they were very drunk, their condition would warrant Clark's allegation that they were "unable to flee"; if their intoxication had reached the surly or quarrelsome stage, the tragedy explains itself.

It may occur to you that a political aroma hangs about that deposition of Benjamin and Rachel Cooper. That

That they prevaricated through inadvertence or design respecting the ages of Winship and Wyman, we must regretfully admit. In view of this fact, are we justified in accepting the balance of their assertions, particularly such as have reference to the number, condition, activities, and armament of guests upon their premises? The tavern stood within the limits of a battle-field, three Britons had just been killed within a few rods of the door, and while we shall never know just what happened within the house, most assuredly in that war-like atmosphere non-combatants, drunk or sober, would have been allowed scant time in which to prove their innocence. The affair at the Cooper Tavern has long been cherished as authority for that sweeping charge of the Reverend Jonas Clark, "the unarmed, the aged and infirm, who are unable to flee, are inhumanly stabbed and murdered in their habitations." * The names of Jason Winship and Jabez Wyman are now inscribed with that of William Marcy upon the monument erected in Cambridge to honor those "who fell in the defence of the Liberty of the People, April 19, 1775."

Finally, some mention must be made of Jason Russell, of Menotomy, if for no other reason, because he with Winship and Wyman was in the mind of the Rev. Jonas Clark when he uttered the lament I have just quoted. Russell was fifty-eight years of age and is said to have been lame. Until the middle of the nine-

* See p. 103, above.

teenth

teenth century he was generally referred to as a helpless bystander, an infirm victim of British brutality. Since that time he has been placed, where he doubtless belongs, in the ranks of the brave and determined men who opposed the King's troops in arms. Singularly enough, this change of status has in no way abated the persistence of the allegation that he "was barbarously murdered in his own house, by Gage's bloody troops."* If he was a slaughtered innocent, well and good; but if a combatant, he is entitled to the honors of a soldier, dead.

The story of Jason Russell is briefly this. He started across the fields to conduct his family to a place of safety, but he left them by the way, and returned to his house alone. "He barricaded his gate with bundles of shingles, making what he thought would be a good cover from which to fire on the enemy as they returned."† Ammi Cutter sought to dissuade him from his purpose, but he refused to leave, declaring that "an Englishman's house was his castle."‡ A party of the Essex militia, who were "unsuspiciously lying in wait" at this point, were surprised by the flank guard and took hasty refuge in Russell's house. Jason Russell was shot as he was entering the door, and the troops followed, "killing all they found inside, save a few who

* From the inscription on the old stone in the precinct burying-ground, said to have been written by the Reverend Mr. Cooke.

† S. A. Smith, *West Cambridge on the Nineteenth of April, 1775*, pp. 37–38.

‡ Cutter, *History of Arlington*, p. 69.

fled

fled to the cellar, the latter shooting whoever of the British attempted to descend the cellar stairs."* Unless we are prepared to assert that every shot fired and every wound inflicted by the British was a wanton atrocity, I think we may dignify the memory of stout-hearted Jason Russell by declaring that he fell in battle in defence of a cause that was more to him than life.

Is Percy guilty or not guilty of the charge of instigating or abetting a system of savagery on his retreat? I admit that I find nothing to support such a charge, either in our knowledge of the man, or in the American evidence that is offered in support of the indictment. That he embittered the fighting after taking over the command is indisputable, but only in the same sense that Grant embittered the fighting in Virginia as compared with the standards of McClellan. He knew nothing of the cases of Raymond, Marcy, or Barber, of Hannah Adams, Jason Russell, or the two men at the Cooper Tavern. We may be sure that he ordered buildings to be fired, or instructed his officers to burn them, as military circumstances required. He must have known of the looting, and it is preposterous to suppose that he did not adopt through his officers the most strenuous measures to break it up. He could have known little of the petty details of the fighting, but he kept the column moving at its even, steady pace, and, in spite of irritating circumstances and some unavoidable confusion, brought it over Charlestown Common on

* Cutter, *History of Arlington*, p. 69.

schedule

schedule time, with about forty killed and only six men missing.

Unlike Colonel Smith, he carried away no bitter memories of the day and harbored no resentment against his enemies for the methods they employed. In fact, he highly commended their tactics as admirably adapted to their purpose. He had believed the people to be cowards and had so expressed himself in letters to his father. After Lexington he frankly confessed his error. "Whoever looks upon them as an irregular mob will find himself much mistaken" is his comment to General Harvey. "For my part, I never believed, I confess, that they would have attacked the King's troops, or have had the perseverance I found in them yesterday." * In *Almon's Remembrancer*, in 1775, there appeared this bit of Boston gossip: "Lord Percy said at table, he never saw anything equal to the intrepidity of the New England minute men." † I should like to feel that there was sitting at the same table that other soldier who remarked, "the rebels were monstrous numerous, and surrounded us on every side; ... but they never would engage us properly." ‡ We know what Percy's reply would have been to that, for we have it in his letters: "they knew too well what was proper, to do so. . . . They have men amongst them who know very well what they are about." §

* April 20, 1775, in *Letters*, p. 52.
† *Remembrancer*, 1775, vol. 1, p. 80.
‡ *Force*, 4th Series, vol. 2, p. 441.
§ April 20, 1775, in *Letters*, pp. 52, 53.

The

The comments of Percy's officers, while less sportsmanlike than those of their chief, are for the most part free from criticism of the tactics employed by their enemy on the 19th of April. Evelyn still insisted that the Provincials were cowards, but sustained by a mad fanatical zeal; while Captain George Harris, afterwards Lord Harris of Indian fame, expressed a wish to meet the Americans in a fair stand-up fight and give them the drubbing they deserved.* Aside from these we find no trace of rancor in the battle narratives of the King's officers. To my mind, these officers, from their commander down, conducted the retreat in the spirit of gentlemen, and not of brutes. As long as war is war, and nations and peoples continue to assert their just or fancied rights by force of arms, I think we may regard the story of Earl Percy's march, in its incitements to barbarities and in its freedom from such excesses upon either side, as a creditable chapter in the military annals of the Anglo-Saxon race.

In conclusion, despite his faults and misdemeanors, I can almost find it in my heart to say a kind word for the British common soldier. I wonder if, after the lapse of nearly one hundred and fifty years, it would be sacrilege to include the name of Thomas Atkins in the list of the heroic sufferers of the day. He had undergone trials that were long and sore, he had been insulted and his uniform reviled, he had encountered

* S. R. Lushington, *Life and Services of General Lord Harris* (1845), p. 40.

New

New England rum, and for resulting offences he had been rigorously punished by his officers. He went out on an excursion through the King's dominions, he was upon the King's business, and was affronted by armed men who denied the King's authority. He had marched and toiled to the last ounce of his strength, and believed that he had been made the victim of sneaking, scalping assassins who were afraid to show their faces. It was a far cry from the military ethics of the French Guard at Fontenoy to those of these rebels of kindred blood. He did not know that he was contending with unselfish patriots who were risking all in a righteous cause, who were willing to die that liberty might live. As, footsore and weary, he strode manfully along, nursing that wicked bayonet of his, and devoid of all compassion toward his foe, we should at least remember that he had suffered much, that he was very brave, and that he did not understand.

THE END